KINDERGARTEN and the COMMON CORE

It's as Easy as ABC!

BY
KATHY BROWN AND
SARAH MARTINO

🍎 Maupin House *by*
capstone®
professional

Kindergarten and the Common Core: It's as Easy as ABC!
By Kathy Brown and Sarah Martino

Cover Design and Cover Artwork: Sandra D'Antonio
Interior Design: Jodi Pedersen

Library of Congress Cataloging-in-Publication Data
Brown, Kathy.
Kindergarten and the common core : it's as easy as ABC /
by Kathy Brown and Sarah Martino.—First edition.
pages cm
includes bibliographical references.
ISBN 978-1-62521-506-2 (pbk.)
1. Kindergarten—United States. 2. Education, Elementary—Standards—United States.
3. Kindergarten—Curricula—United States. I. Title.
LB1205.B76 2014
372.21'8—dc23   2013043877

Maupin House publishes professional resources for K–12 educators.
Contact us for tailored, in-school training or to schedule an author for a workshop or conference.
Visit www.maupinhouse.com for free lesson plan downloads.

Maupin House Publishing, Inc. by Capstone Professional
1710 Roe Crest Drive
North Mankato, MN 56003
www.maupinhouse.com
888-262-6135
info@maupinhouse.com

Printed in the United States of America in Eau Claire, Wisconsin.
012014   007955

Acknowledgments

Writing is such a catalyst for reflection! Pondering our thoughts about teaching the Common Core Standards has caused us to examine everything we do. We have learned much about ourselves as educators, collaborators, and friends!

First, we want to thank our precious students. Kindergartners exude infinite amounts of energy and enthusiasm. Their eagerness to learn motivates us daily to be the best we can be. We are so lucky to be part of such wonderful kindergarten learning families!

Additionally, we want to recognize the Salzmanns for all of their support. Thanks for encouraging us to always dream big and for supporting us every step of the way!

To our friends Catherine Johansen and Lynnette Brent, thanks for your wisdom in being able to see the big picture. You are amazingly articulate and bright women. We will be forever grateful for the connections you have made for us and for your friendships!

Thanks to Capstone and Maupin House for this opportunity to share our thoughts about the wonderful world of kindergarten. We must especially recognize Karen Soll, who has taken us by the hand and led us through the process. Your guidance has been crucial in helping us create a book that will hopefully be a useful resource for many kindergarten teachers.

To our families, thanks so very much from the bottom of our hearts for your love, patience, and encouragement throughout this process. You have always been our biggest cheerleaders! You are appreciated and loved immensely!

TABLE OF CONTENTS

Foreword

As a teacher trained to teach middle and high school, kindergarten was a mystery to me. Informed mostly by my own experiences, I pictured kindergarten as a place with milk and cookies, nap time, shoe-tying, jacket-zipping, grubby hands—a great place to visit, but I wouldn't leave my seventh graders to stay there.

Then something changed my thinking. One of my most trusted friends, Catherine Johansen, kept telling me that I had to meet "these teachers." These teachers were doing groundbreaking things in kindergarten classrooms. These teachers were state-of-the-art literacy instructors whose students were reading and writing on day one. These teachers brought both rigor and engagement to kids and helped parents understand their children's development as learners. That was my introduction to Kathy Brown and Sarah Martino, "these teachers" who finally helped me understand the magic and the immense potential and importance of kindergarten.

We all met at a coffee shop. We took over a back room and spread curriculum materials across tables, and they sang to me! After getting over the initial shock of the public singing of "What Do You Like that Begins with *S*?" I thought, "How could a child not love to be in their class?"

So I went to observe in their rooms, and I was in awe of the energy. When Kathy and Sarah asked the kids, "Can you read it?" the children yelled back, "Yes we can!" And, I have to admit it, I joined in the chant. The enthusiasm and the love of learning were that contagious.

I am thrilled that in my role at Capstone Professional, I can help bring the words and work of Sarah and Kathy to life. I'm honored to be their friend. Packed between the covers of this volume is a true love of children and of learning, a deep understanding of content and standards—and the wisdom it takes to pull it all together. Kathy and Sarah have a knack for making kindergarten both rigorous and magical. They create an atmosphere where children feel comfortable taking the risks that help them grow as readers, writers, and thinkers. They help parents understand what their children are capable of doing in kindergarten, and they tie it back to standards. Their love of their job touches every listener who hears them speak, each parent who is lucky enough to have a child in their class, and each child who walks through their doors and leaves at the end of the year brimming with enthusiasm and confidence.

This resource is a must-read for any teacher who wants to transform his or her kindergarten classroom into an incredible community of learners, a room steeped in best practices with undeniable excitement. Kathy and Sarah's voices come through loud and clear, and their work will inspire your teaching. I know they inspired me.

Lynnette R. Brent
Capstone

CHAPTER 1

CREATING A MAGICAL KINDERGARTEN ENVIRONMENT: Empowering Our Youngest Learners

> Walking through the door with clutched hands, parents and children alike were wide-eyed and filled with anxiety. Neither the tears nor the stoic smiles could hide their feelings of reluctance to let go. The first day of kindergarten marks an amazing milestone in each child's educational journey. As kindergarten teachers, we are charged with the overwhelming responsibility to reach out and embrace each precious hand and guide each child through the gateway to extraordinary learning.

Embracing the Challenges Surrounding Common Core in Kindergarten

Kindergarten now symbolizes the first time in a child's life when learning expectations are clearly defined by the Common Core Standards. The adoption of the rigorous Common Core Standards has created a unique challenge for the teachers of our youngest learners. The tremendous task currently facing kindergarten teachers is how to create developmentally appropriate environments that simultaneously meet new academic demands.

Kindergarten is undoubtedly different. Unlike other grade levels, kindergarten programs vary in length and structure across states, districts, and even schools. In fact, kindergarten is not mandated in many states. Districts that do offer kindergarten can create their own policies defining entrance age eligibility, length of school day, materials, and class size. "These variations can dramatically alter the opportunities for young children to meet expectations identified by the Common Core." (Snow 2012)

This lack of consistency has created stress among kindergarten teachers. Some teachers have two hours to meet student needs while others are afforded a full day. Some teachers have 15 students while others have more than 30. Despite these discrepancies, we are all mandated to have our students meet the same end-of-the-year kindergarten expectations.

We also must not forget that kindergarten is caught in the crossroads of education. It lies between early childhood learning and the intensified demands of primary education. With good intentions, we want to protect our students' social and emotional development from a rigid, developmentally inappropriate, skill-and-drill based classroom. Thus, we need to overcome these challenges by providing a strong foundation for learning that is developmentally appropriate and can be implemented in any kindergarten structure.

Further heightening the anxiety surrounding the Common Core Standards is the reality that many districts are evaluating teachers on student growth aligned to the standards. Rightfully so, it would be easy for exhausted kindergarten teachers to say, "we can't" to the Common Core. We challenge you to find inspiration from the beloved children's classic *The Little Engine that Could.* The big engines failed because they didn't believe in themselves and the power of positive thinking. We encourage you to embrace the Common Core Standards as the little blue engine would by finding the little voice inside of you that whispers that you can do it.

Developmentally Appropriate Practices

Kindergarten should be a journey, not a race. As kindergarten teachers, we want to fill that journey with as much fun and progress as possible. The ultimate goal would be to help students become empowered learners who successfully apply information to a variety of real-life situations. Too often, we unintentionally focus on coverage of content rather than teaching a deeper understanding of learning.

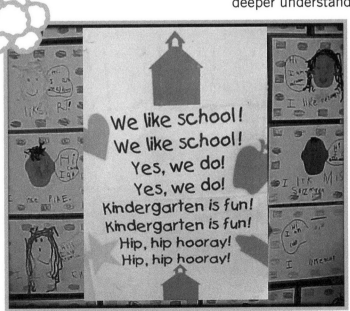

Taking children on a journey of learning means providing them with daily opportunities to solve problems, interact with peers, and build confidence. Simply rushing to memorize facts does not inspire curiosity or higher-level thinking. Instead, learning is viewed as a means to an end rather than a joyful journey filled with song, dance, humor, dialogue, engagement, exploration, enthusiasm, celebration, and reflection. Learning for young children must be active and social in nature. In its position statement on developmentally appropriate practice, NAEYC (2009) states "Children are thinking, moving, feeling and interacting human beings. To teach them well involves considering and fostering their development and learning in all domains. Children's development and learning in one domain is influenced by what takes place in other domains."

These domains include the physical, intellectual, emotional, and social needs of young children. When reflecting upon the development of young learners, kindergarten teachers need to view their students as "**PIES**." (See Figure 1.1.)

- P-Physical
- I-Intellectual
- E-Emotional
- S-Social

Figure 1.1 PIES Chart

Teachers need to examine the whole child carefully and set goals that create well-rounded learners. Often, students enter kindergarten with strengths and weaknesses in very specific areas. It is crucial for kindergarten teachers to be aware of every child's individual level of development in each domain. Differentiated goals can be set based on student strengths and weaknesses. The ultimate objective is to have a classroom full of well-rounded PIES.

Johnny entered kindergarten just turning five years old. Intellectually, he was very advanced with an extensive vocabulary, knowledge of letters and sounds, and the ability to begin to read sight words. He had an amazing attention span and followed routines successfully. He was friendly and played well with peers. However, Johnny struggled with fine motor tasks, such as zipping, buttoning, cutting, writing, coloring, etc. When faced with these challenges, Johnny withdrew from the group, pushed his paper off the table, and exhibited extreme frustration. Johnny needed to further develop in the physical and emotional domains of PIES. When his mother inquired about having Johnny be moved to the first grade, it was helpful to have analyzed his development. First, we celebrated his strengths in intellectual and social skills. Next, we were able to collaborate in setting goals for his physical (fine motor) and emotional (frustration) skills. Mom quickly realized that the kindergarten classroom would be the most appropriate environment to meet his needs. We could build on his strengths and work on his weaknesses.

A truly developmentally appropriate classroom must focus on each student's needs and interests and celebrate his or her diversity. In addition to knowing the domains, a kindergarten teacher must make the effort to gather information about each student. Kindergarten teachers do not have the luxury of a previous elementary school teacher to provide crucial background information. Parents should be utilized to share information about their child's interests, talents, and home life. Have parents complete

Kindergarten Information Sheets, such as Figures 1.2 and 1.3. Forging a partnership of communication with parents is essential in getting to know each child before he or she enters school.

Effective teachers use student background information to inspire, ignite excitement, and establish a relationship of trust and respect. When teachers create an atmosphere of warmth, love, and acceptance, kindergartners feel valued and are motivated to take risks in learning.

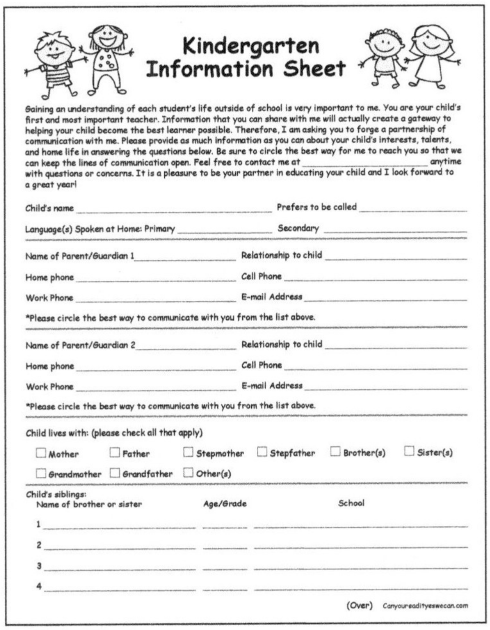

Kindergarten Information Sheet

Gaining an understanding of each student's life outside of school is very important to me. You are your child's first and most important teacher. Information that you can share with me will actually create a gateway to helping your child become the best learner possible. Therefore, I am asking you to forge a partnership of communication with me. Please provide as much information as you can about your child's interests, talents, and home life in answering the questions below. Be sure to circle the best way for me to reach you so that we can keep the lines of communication open. Feel free to contact me at ____________ anytime with questions or concerns. It is a pleasure to be your partner in educating your child and I look forward to a great year!

Child's name ____________ Prefers to be called ____________

Language(s) Spoken at Home: Primary ____________ Secondary ____________

Name of Parent/Guardian 1 ____________ Relationship to child ____________

Home phone ____________ Cell Phone ____________

Work Phone ____________ E-mail Address ____________

*Please circle the best way to communicate with you from the list above.

Name of Parent/Guardian 2 ____________ Relationship to child ____________

Home phone ____________ Cell Phone ____________

Work Phone ____________ E-mail Address ____________

*Please circle the best way to communicate with you from the list above.

Child lives with: (please check all that apply)

☐ Mother ☐ Father ☐ Stepmother ☐ Stepfather ☐ Brother(s) ☐ Sister(s)

☐ Grandmother ☐ Grandfather ☐ Other(s)

Child's siblings:

Name of brother or sister	Age/Grade	School
1		
2		
3		
4		

(Over) Canyoureadityeswecan.com

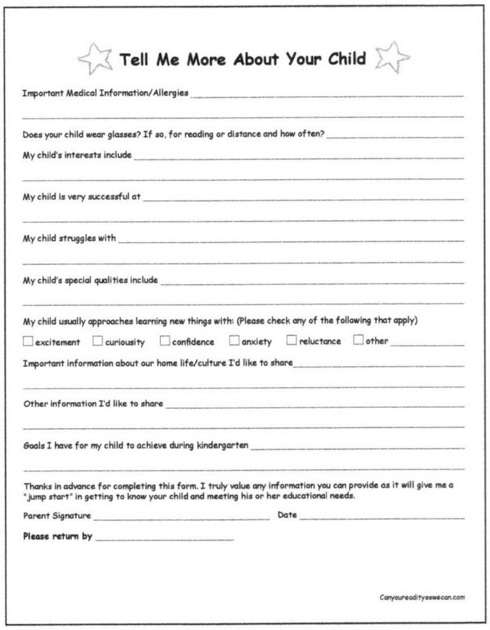

Tell Me More About Your Child

Important Medical Information/Allergies ____________

Does your child wear glasses? If so, for reading or distance and how often? ____________

My child's interests include ____________

My child is very successful at ____________

My child struggles with ____________

My child's special qualities include ____________

My child usually approaches learning new things with: (Please check any of the following that apply)

☐ excitement ☐ curiousity ☐ confidence ☐ anxiety ☐ reluctance ☐ other ____________

Important information about our home life/culture I'd like to share ____________

Other information I'd like to share ____________

Goals I have for my child to achieve during kindergarten ____________

Thanks in advance for completing this form. I truly value any information you can provide as it will give me a "jump start" in getting to know your child and meeting his or her educational needs.

Parent Signature ____________ Date ____________

Please return by ____________

Canyoureadityeswecan.com

Figures1.2 and 1.3 Kindergarten Information Sheet
Full pages available in Appendix

In a position statement about developmentally appropriate practices, NAEYC (2009) has expressed concerns that standards overload has created "schools that are curtailing valuable experiences such as problem solving, rich play, collaboration of peers, opportunities for emotional and social development, outdoor/physical activity and the arts." Keep this in mind as you choose the most appropriate activities that effectively embed Common Core instruction into developmentally appropriate practices. It is essential to believe that kindergartners can learn any content as long as it is taught with methods that respect our youngest learners. Play-based learning encompasses all areas of development and is therefore the ultimate example of developmentally appropriate practice. Children who are engaged in play are active physically, intellectually, emotionally, and socially as they solve problems and interact with their peers. Play is the epitome of developmentally appropriate practice. Play fills the classroom with vibrancy, enthusiasm, enjoyment, and fun and learning is most effective this way.

Role-playing is an effective strategy that associates play with learning. Role-playing combines thought and action and encourages expression. It helps children develop socially, emotionally, and intellectually. Reading books like *If I Were an Astronaut, If I Were the President, If I Were a Ballerina,* and others in the Picture Window Series published by Capstone can serve as a springboard for social studies lessons. Children can describe different careers using role-play. For instance, Mitchell wanted to be a firefighter. First, he dressed up for the part. Then, he engaged in collaborative conversations with his peers about firefighters and the role they play in the community. Next, he became a firefighter and shared this role-play with the class. By participating in the activity, he was able to demonstrate several of the speaking and listening Common Core Standards. As an extension he wrote a story to go with his photograph of being a firefighter. After writing his story, he proudly shared his work in the Author's Chair.

Build the Kindergarten Family and a Community of Confident Learners

It is of utmost importance to construct a kindergarten family that cares for each other and values differences while maintaining a focus on learning. Norms should be set for social interaction and engaged learning in order to create a risk-taking environment where mistakes are not stumbling blocks but opportunities for learning. To envision a kindergarten family is to imagine a collaborative community where everyone is committed to helping one another learn. Participation is encouraged by all, and respect exudes from students and teachers alike. Diversity, the willingness to try, encouragement, and celebration define the truly effective kindergarten family. Cultivate a classroom characterized by combining these critical elements and a magical kindergarten environment will follow.

Imagine sitting in front of your class on the first day of school. "Kindergartners, isn't it so exciting to be together at school? Did you know that every day we are going to be together just like a learning family? Your parents have a job to do every day. They might go to an office to do work or they might work at home. Now that you are in kindergarten you have a job to do too. Your job is to come to school and learn. There are so many of you that we have to have rules so that we can all do our best at school. Can you think of a rule that would help us do our best?"

Encourage students to turn and talk to a friend and share their ideas. Listen and supply feedback to keep them on task. Have students share a few ideas as you construct an anchor chart entitled "Kindergarten Family." Steer children toward creating good norms.

Consistently praise students for demonstrating the desired behavior. For example, I might say, "Wow, Logan! You made my heart so happy when you wrote me that note telling me that I was the best teacher in the whole world. People in a kindergarten family say nice things to each other all the time."

This is a co-constructed Kindergarten Family Anchor Chart.

Building a kindergarten family creates a community of confident learners. A child's success in school is enhanced when the classroom environment is comfortable and safe. When children feel safe, they are more likely to explore their curiosities. In turn, they have a greater opportunity to climb higher on the ladder to learning. If they believe that they can learn, then they truly will. Bardige and Segals (2005) support this philosophy: "Children's belief in themselves as learners and their eagerness to learn new things is grounded in their early conversations with the people who are important in their lives." Good teachers strive to be one of those people.

Exude Excitement and Enthusiasm

Young children thrive in a joyful learning environment. Use strategies that exude enthusiasm. An energetic and excited kindergarten teacher who projects a love for learning encourages students to approach each new learning task with equal excitement. Keep in mind that 5 and 6 year olds are extremely egocentric and innately motivated by praise. Capitalize on creating challenging yet achievable goals for your students. Consistently celebrate success. Even a small taste of success can inspire a kindergartner to take risks and become an independent learner.

During teachable moments, intentionally direct the learning community's awareness to children who display appropriate behaviors and mastery of skills. Recognize these accomplishments with mini celebrations, including clapping, creating special cheers, or having the successful student sign his or her name on a superstar chart. When you catch students making good choices, it will make their buttons burst with pride.

Use chanting as another strategy to help students develop a positive attitude toward learning. Simply ask your kindergartners, "Can you do it?" and teach them to respond with, "Yes we can!" It is amazing how positive persuasion can be in empowering confident learners. If kindergartners believe they can, they will. Creating this atmosphere allows each child to develop a sense of wonder and curiosity that is motivated by enthusiasm. Enthusiasm is the hook that reels in a young child's desire to learn.

Superstar Listener Chart

Imagine kindergartners sitting on the carpet and all of them want to tell you something at the same time. Owen is sitting quietly waiting for his turn. He is demonstrating the behaviors of a superstar listener by keeping his hands in his lap, his eyes on the teacher, and his voice quiet. Promote this behavior by catching Owen doing the right thing.

"Owen, I am so proud of you. I just caught you being a superstar listener. Class, let's give Owen some fireworks." Pause for class celebration. "I hope I can catch some more friends keeping their hands to themselves and their eyes on the speaker. Boys and girls, I love it when you are good listeners because it helps us all be able to learn. Owen, you have earned the privilege of putting your name on the Superstar Listener chart. We are all proud of you."

Don't overlook the importance of modeling. Kindergartners lack prior experiences and knowledge, so they require new content to be modeled in concrete ways. Strive to strike the perfect balance between scaffolding and expecting independence. Great teachers know when to provide modeling and when to stretch students to explore learning autonomously.

You can do this with a gradual release of responsibility model. First, instill enthusiasm by capturing students' interests and building their self-esteem. Next, carefully model lesson expectations. Then, allow students in small groups to independently practice expectations while you circulate and provide corrective feedback. Last, encourage students to meet the expectations independently. Apply this teaching routine to all instructional scenarios. This strategy is effective when used to teach writing, turn and talks, reading strategies, problem solving, and so on as well as for classroom management. The ultimate reward reaped from modeling is learners who are confidently engaged in reading, writing, speaking, and listening in an effort to make sense of their world.

You can also empower your youngest learners with purposeful planning and intentionality. Effective teachers are intentional in everything they do and say. NAEYC (2009) states, "Intentional teachers are purposeful and thoughtful about the actions they take, and they direct their teaching toward the goals the program is trying to help children reach." Instill the magic in your classroom by clearly defining your end goals and intentionally aligning your planning to achieve these goals.

The classroom is your stage to set for student success. You can create a magical developmentally appropriate classroom that functions as a kindergarten family, exudes excitement, works collaboratively, and creates confident learners. Keep these items in mind when setting your stage:

- Arrange the physical space in your classroom to encourage collaboration.

- Provide places for small group, whole group, and independent activities.

- Surround the children with a print-rich environment and anchor charts that guide them to be successful in demonstrating the norms of the classroom.

- Establish areas for play and exploration that are aligned to content areas (science center, reading corner, math manipulatives, a learning shelf filled with games, computer center, listening center, and so on).

- Display kid-friendly learning goals to create an atmosphere of engaged, focused learning.

- Encourage risk-taking and celebrate success.

- Purposefully plan activities that facilitate growth of the whole child (PIES).

- Show a genuine concern and value for each child's needs and interests.

- Forge powerful parent partnerships.

- Scaffold learning to ensure success.

- Exude enthusiasm for learning, as it is contagious!

Once your stage is set, implementing the Common Core Standards is as easy as ABC!

Aha Moments:
Snippets for Reflection

★ The tremendous task currently facing kindergarten teachers is how to create developmentally appropriate environments that simultaneously meet new academic demands.

★ Kindergarten is caught in the crossroads of education. It lies between early childhood learning and the intensified demands of primary education.

★ Challenges may be overcome by providing a strong foundation for learning that is developmentally appropriate and can be implemented in any kindergarten structure.

★ The ultimate goal is to create students who are empowered learners and can successfully apply information to a variety of real-life situations.

★ Children should be taken on a journey of learning that involves daily opportunities to solve problems, interact with peers, and build confidence.

★ Teachers must be aware of every child's individual level of development in each domain.

★ A truly developmentally appropriate classroom must focus on each student's needs and interests and celebrate his or her diversity.

★ A partnership of communication with parents is essential in getting to know each child before he or she enters school.

★ Student background information should be used to inspire, create excitement, and establish a relationship of trust and respect.

★ Kindergartners can learn any content as long as it is instructed with methods that respect their learning.

★ Play is the epitome of a developmentally appropriate practice.

★ A kindergarten family cares for each other and values differences while maintaining a focus on learning.

★ Mistakes are not stumbling blocks but opportunities for learning.

★ Diversity, the willingness to try, encouragement, and celebration define the truly effective kindergarten family.

★ A child's success in school is enhanced with a classroom environment that is comfortable and safe.

★ Enthusiasm is the hook that can reel in a young child's desire to learn.

★ The goal should be the perfect balance between scaffolding and expecting independence.

★ Kindergartners should be inspired by consistently celebrating success.

★ The learning community should be made aware of children who display appropriate behaviors and mastery of skills.

★ It is amazing how positive persuasion can empower confident learners.

★ The ultimate reward reaped from modeling is learners who are confidently engaged in reading, writing, speaking, and listening in an effort to make sense of their world.

★ The essential hallmark of effective teaching is intentionality.

CHAPTER 2

CRACKING THE CODE: Making Sense of the Common Core Standards

The Life of a Kindergarten Teacher

Teaching is such hard work. In what other profession do you have 25 unique clients all demanding something different daily? Yet, you have to meet all of their needs and the needs of their families by yourself at the same time every day and in the same setting. You have to show documentation, provide consistent feedback, and monitor progress regularly. You can't go to the bathroom or take a break anytime between 8–3. Don't even think about making a personal phone call or scheduling an appointment during the week. You eat when you can and if you have to take a day off, plan on staying at least an extra hour the night before. You are a doctor, a referee, a mom, a dad, a housekeeper, a motivator, an actor, a supervisor, a problem solver, a statistician, a caregiver, a lecturer, a mentor, a salesman, and an event planner.

You are a kindergarten teacher.

Overview of the Common Core English Language Arts Standards

Teaching is undoubtedly one the most challenging professions. The addition of the Common Core Standards brings even more apprehension. It is important to examine the Common Core Standards through a positive lens and realize that there are limited differences between past standards and the current Common Core. As stated in its Mission Statement, "The Common Core State Standards provide a consistent, clear understanding of what students are expected to learn, so teachers and parents know what

This kindergartner is engaged in play while demonstrating application of standard K.RF.3c.

they need to do to help them." The statement further reveals that the standards are designed to be robust and relevant to the real world, reflecting the knowledge and skills that our young people need for success in college and careers. The English Language Arts (ELA) standards are intended to be rigorous and concise to ensure that all stakeholders have a clear understanding of the expectations in reading, writing, speaking, listening, and language. The standards encourage equity by ensuring all students, regardless of demographics, are equipped with the skills necessary to compete in a global economy.

The vision for student achievement is defined by the Common Core Standards, but methods of instruction are not dictated. The standards call for a deeper understanding of knowledge. They demand an evidence-based application of content through higher-level thinking skills. We must focus on creating engaging atmospheres that encourage application of knowledge versus simple skill and drill.

You can intentionally plan for instruction in the same manner you would approach completing a jigsaw puzzle. First, envision the complete puzzle to gain guidance in how to effectively connect pieces. Only then can you truly see how the individual pieces can be carefully woven together to maximize student achievement. The interconnectedness of the ELA standards can help to create classrooms that are focused on reading, writing, speaking, listening, and language. Avoid looking at each standard in isolation as it causes teachers to feel overwhelmed and instruction to be disconnected. The standards need to be embraced as building blocks rather than stumbling blocks.

How to Read the Standards

Reading the standards can be confusing if you don't know how to "crack the code." First, it is important to know that there are six learning content strands in the ELA Standards. These strands include Reading Standards: Literature (RL), Reading Standards: Informational Text (RI), Reading Standards: Foundational Skills (RF), Writing Standards (W), Speaking and Listening Standards (SL), and Language Standards (L).

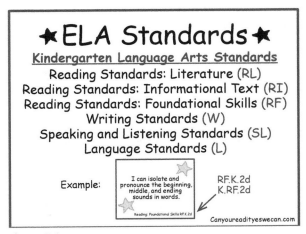

Figure 2.1

Each strand consists of multiple standards that are numbered. Some standards contain additional learning targets designated by a letter. For example, in Figure 2.1, the strand shown is Reading Standards: Foundational Skills (RF). The standard that is chosen is the second in the strand, "Demonstrate the understanding of spoken words, syllables, and sounds." It is further narrowed to "d," which is "isolate and pronounce the initial, medial vowel, and final sounds in three-phoneme words." The code for this particular standard can be written K.RF.2d or RF.K.2d. Some educators put the grade level first while others begin with the strand. It is simply as easy as learning the acronyms for the standards and no different than learning abbreviations like IEP or RTI. Being able to "crack the code" will help you navigate through the standards seamlessly. You have been teaching these standards for years. It is just a matter of aligning the language of the Common Core Standards to what you currently teach. You will be relieved by how easy it is to make a direct correlation between your current classroom targets and the Common Core Standards. Also, note that the ELA standards present a greater demand for children to be able to read text with higher complexity. In order to account for this shift in expectations, you will need to provide students with more opportunities to be engaged in authentic reading and writing with increasingly challenging text.

How to Use Kid-Friendly Standards

It is a worthwhile endeavor to rewrite the standards in a kid-friendly language to spark instant connections with staff and students. For example, notice how complicated the following standard reads in its original language: "Read common high-frequency words by sight (e.g., the, of, to, you, she, my, is, are, do, does)." Kindergarten students would have a difficult time making meaning from the vocabulary used in that standard. You can rewrite it in kid-friendly language as, "I can read sight words."

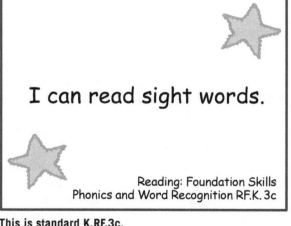

I can read sight words.

Reading: Foundation Skills
Phonics and Word Recognition RF.K.3c

This is standard K.RF.3c.
It can also be written as RF.K.3c.

I can name and recognize all capital and lowercase letters of the alphabet.

Reading: Foundation Skills Print Concepts RF.K.1d

This is standard K.RF.1d.
It can also be written as RF.K.1d.

It is obviously easier for young students to be able to comprehend the kid-friendly standards as they truly speak their language. Kid-friendly standards also streamline focus, allowing students to connect to the essential part of each standard. Taking the time to strip away the unnecessary technical language will pay dividends later as you create a learning community where all stakeholders are standards-focused.

Don't underestimate the potential of kid-friendly standards in empowering your work. A printed list of kid-friendly standards can be powerful as a reference tool when lesson planning. (See Figures 2.2 and 2.3.) You will clearly see the alignment of instruction to the Common Core Standards when the technical language is removed. Keeping a kid-friendly list at your fingertips also allows for easy documentation of the standards you are incorporating into your daily instruction. When teachers become immersed in the kid-friendly language, everyone speaks the same language and a classroom culture of standards-focused learning can be created.

Kindergarten
☆ English Language Arts Standards ☆

Reading Standards: Literature

RL.K.1	I can ask and answer questions about text.
RL.K.2	I can retell stories with details.
RL.K.3	I can identify characters, setting, and major events in a story.
RL.K.4	I can ask and answer questions about words I do not know.
RL.K.5	I can recognize common types of text.
RL.K.6	I can identify the author and illustrator and describe what they do.
RL.K.7	I can match the illustration with its written part in the story.
RL.K.8	(does not apply)
RL.K.9	I can compare story characters and events.
RL.K.10	I can participate in group reading activities.

Reading Standards: Informational Text

RI.K.1	I can ask and answer questions about informational text.
RI.K.2	I can identify the main idea and give details of the text.
RI.K.3	I can describe connections between individuals, events, and information in a text.
RI.K.4	I can ask and answer questions about words I do not know in text.
RI.K.5	I can identify the front cover, back cover, and title page of a book.
RI.K.6	I can identify the author and illustrator and describe what they do.
RI.K.7	I can match the illustration with its written part in the story.
RI.K.8	I can find evidence in a text to support the author's main idea.
RI.K.9	I can identify similarities and differences in texts.
RI.K.10	I can participate in group reading activities.

Reading Standards: Foundational Skills

RF.K.1	I can show you how books work.
RF.K.1a	I can follow words from left to right, top to bottom, and page by page.
RF.K.1b	I know that words are written by using specific letters.
RF.K.1c	I know that words are separated by spaces in print.
RF.K.1d	I can name and recognize all capital and lowercase letters of the alphabet.
RF.K.2	I can play with words, syllables, and sounds.
RF.K.2a	I can tell you if two words rhyme, and I can make a rhyming word.
RF.K.2b	I can count, pronounce, blend, and segment syllables in words.
RF.K.2c	I can break apart and blend words using onsets and rimes.
RF.K.2d	I can isolate and pronounce the beginning, middle, and ending sounds in a word.
RF.K.2e	I can change beginning, middle, or ending sounds to make new words.
RF.K.3	I can decode words.
RF.K.3a	I can say the consonant letter sounds.
RF.K.3b	I can say the two sounds a vowel makes.
RF.K.3c	I can read sight words.
RF.K.3d	I can identify the letter sound that is different in words with similar spellings.
RF.K.4	I can read and make meaning.

Writing Standards

W.K.1	I can write about my opinion about a book or topic.
W.K.2	I can write to give information about a topic.
W.K.3	I can write about an event or a series of events.
	(There is no W.K.4 standard as it starts in Grade 3)
W.K.5	I can edit my writing to make it better.
W.K.6	I can use digital tools to write.
W.K.7	I can participate in shared research and writing about a topic.
W.K.8	I can answer questions through remembering experiences and information.

Speaking and Listening Standards

SL.K.1	I know how to be a superstar listener and speaker.
SL.K.1a	I can show that I am a superstar listener and speaker.
SL.K.1b	I take turns listening and speaking.
SL.K.2	I can ask and answer questions to help me understand information presented in ways other than by a speaker.
SL.K.3	I can ask and answer questions to help me understand information presented by a speaker.
SL.K.4	I can describe people, places, things, and events and give details.
SL.K.5	I can add drawings and pictures to make my presentations more understandable.
SL.K.6	I can be a superstar speaker.

Language Standards

L.K.1	I am a superstar speaker and a superstar writer.
L.K.1a	I can write my capital and lowercase letters.
L.K.1b	I can speak and write using correct nouns and verbs.
L.K.1c	I can speak and write using correct plurals.
L.K.1d	I can speak and write using correct question words.
L.K.1e	I can speak and write using prepositions.
L.K.1f	I can share ideas in complete sentences.
L.K.2a-d	I can write sentences using capital letters, punctuation, and kindergarten spelling.
L.K.3	(Begins in grade 2)
L.K.4	I can learn the meaning of new words.
L.K.4a	I know that some words can have more than one meaning.
L.K.4b	I can be a detective to look for parts in words to help me understand their meaning.
L.K.5	I know to look for clues when I don't know the meaning of a new word.
L.K.5a	I can sort objects into categories.
L.K.5b	I can identify the opposite of a word.
L.K.5c	I can make connections between words I hear and read to my world.
L.K.5d	I can act out verbs that have similar meanings.
L.K.6	I can learn new words first and then use them in my speaking and writing.

Notes:

Canyoureadityeswecan.com

Figures 2.2 and 2.3 Kid-Friendly List of Standards
Full pages available in Appendix

You can also use kid-friendly standards as an assessment tool. Observation checklists and anecdotal records can be generated to document progress of standards-aligned skills. Carefully create a chart with the names of all of your students in rows on the left. Then list the kid-friendly standards that you wish to assess at the top of each column. (See Figures 2.4 and 2.5.) These tools can be used to assess children as they are engaged in authentic reading and writing activities. Simply put the assessment on a clipboard and walk around your classroom as children are participating in developmentally appropriate centers, such as role-playing, writing center, reading corner, literacy centers, and so on. Place a check mark or date next to the child's name when he or she demonstrates a targeted skill. This will prove to be a phenomenal tool because it not only supplies significant documentation on each learner's progress toward achieving the standards, but it also gathers data in a manner that is authentic and developmentally appropriate. Children are not being asked to demonstrate isolated skills on a worksheet or multiple-choice tests. Instead, they are demonstrating achievement of connected Common Core Standards by being engaged in realistic literacy activities.

Be wise and look at each child as a canvas and the standards as the paint. Be cautious not to splash colors around aimlessly in isolation. Rather, paint an intentional picture where each connected stroke is chosen carefully. We challenge you to be artists in the classroom and craft a Common Core-aligned literacy masterpiece for every student.

Figures 2.4 and 2.5 Kid-Friendly Assessments: Observation Checklists
Full pages available in Appendix

Aha Moments: Snippets for Reflection

★ Common Core Standards should be viewed through a positive lens. Realize that there are limited differences between past standards and the current Common Core.

★ The ELA standards are intended to be rigorous and concise to ensure that all stakeholders have a clear understanding of the expectations in reading, writing, speaking, listening, and language.

★ A shared vision of student achievement is defined by the Common Core Standards, but it does not dictate how teachers should teach.

★ The standards demand an evidence-based application of content through higher-level thinking skills.

★ There are six learning content strands in the ELA Standards. These strands include Reading Standards: Literature (RL), Reading Standards: Informational Text (RI), Reading Standards: Foundational Skills (RF), Writing Standards (W), Speaking and Listening Standards (SL), and Language Standards (L).

★ It is easy to make a direct correlation between your current classroom targets and the Common Core Standards.

★ Students should be provided with more opportunities to be engaged in authentic reading and writing with more challenging text.

★ Standards written in kid-friendly language spark instant connections for staff and students.

★ Kid-friendly standards streamline focus to the part of the standard that describes the truly essential skill.

★ A printed list of kid-friendly standards can be a powerful reference tool when lesson planning.

★ Students and staff who become immersed in kid-friendly standards benefit from speaking the same language.

★ A kid-friendly observation checklist is a great tool because it supplies significant documentation on each learner and gathers data in a manner that is authentic and developmentally appropriate.

CHAPTER 3

ROUTINES:
They're as Easy as ABC

Kindergarten Chaos

It's the first day of kindergarten. Twenty-two 5 year olds enter my door, some with exuberance while others with reluctance. As the kindergarten teacher, I can count on the fact that each has a different perception about what will truly transpire in the wonderful world of kindergarten.

I quickly realize I have lost control when the crowd scatters. Some run to the reading corner in an effort to secure their favorite book. Others rush to the toy shelf to monopolize the Legos while shouting, "These are mine!" It is the tug on my shirt, however, from the child who is too afraid to leave my side that commands my immediate attention. It sounds as if 100 little voices are all speaking at the same time. "I have to go potty." "Can I get a drink?" "Where's my mom?" "Can we go outside?" "What's for lunch?" "Where is my bus?" "Can I see my brother?" "When can we go home?"

Yet, sobbing and sniffling can still be heard above the roar from a few who are too afraid to venture out into the group. As I turn my head, there is Cheyenne crouching as she clutches herself and crosses her legs. I know that could only mean one thing. I shout out, "Cheyenne, do you have to go the bathroom?" As she nervously nods, I point her in the direction of the bathroom. I must reach quickly into my teaching toolbox and re-establish harmony before an all-out mutiny erupts!

Oh, how I need a better routine!

Do You Know Just What to Do? Yes, We Know Just What to Do!

Never underestimate the power of routines. Dedicate yourself to setting routines to ensure student success in navigating their school day. You can't begin to expect students to achieve the rigorous academic skills of the Common Core Standards until they can follow routines. Children lack prior knowledge, thus they thrive on routines from the day they are born. Successful parents innately rely on rituals to help their children grow in making sense of the world around them. Bathroom routines, eating routines, bedtime routines, and dressing routines are the anchors that help young children reach new levels of independence daily. To effectively facilitate learning, capitalize on the use of seamless routines in the same way parents do.

Kindergartners enter our doors without prior knowledge of the elementary school world. Therefore, it is crucial that we create a common ground so that students know what to expect and can be open to new learning. For example, posting a daily schedule can help relieve anxiety. Both children and adults benefit from knowing what is going to happen next. Effective kindergarten schedules combine print and pictures to help children make meaning of their day.

Start each day by referring to the schedule to provide students confidence and purpose. This routine will relieve anxiety so that students are open to new learning. The ultimate goal is for students to independently refer to the schedule as questions arise during their day. Simply by adding a chant such as, "Do you know just what to do?" and asking students to respond with "Yes, we know just what to do!" can inspire instant engagement in a 5 year old. Students will be immediately pumped up with enthusiasm and the deep desire to demonstrate that they know just what to do. Chanting can equate to a recipe for success in motivating student behavior. Use these strategies to shape inexperienced young learners into students who successfully navigate the structure of their day in a stress-free manner.

Another advantage of routines is the comfort level provided to parents. Unique to kindergarten is the extreme apprehension that first-time parents feel about the unknowns of education. The source of their stress is the lack of control they now have in determining their children's daily activities. This fear can be extinguished quickly with intentional teacher-parent communication. Just like their children, parents instantly develop trust in teachers when they can envision a clear picture of the kindergarten routine. This trust translates into increased time focused on learning because minimal time is required to address parent concerns. Families that understand the kindergarten schedule can also better prepare their children for school. Undoubtedly, consistent routines implemented during daily classroom work support a sense of safety, assurance, and trust in all stakeholders.

Introducing the Common Core 3

If you want your entire learning community to understand the Common Core Standards, you must immerse them in the Common Core language. There are three main routines that will help you incorporate the standards into your daily instruction: display, communicate, and integrate. Call this approach the "Common Core 3." These routines, when used together, have proven to be successful in creating awareness of the Common Core Standards in the kindergarten classroom.

The Common Core 3

- ★ <u>Display:</u> standards routinely
- ★ <u>Communicate:</u> standards with parents and students
- ★ <u>Integrate:</u> standards throughout multiple content areas and instructional settings

Canyoureadityeswecan.com

A Learning-Focused Kindergarten Community

The hustle and bustle of the beginning of a school day quickly comes to a halt as the principal's voice is heard through the schoolwide intercom system. He clearly commands attention as he states, "Everyone, please stand for the Pledge of Allegiance." Kindergartners obediently put their hands on their hearts and eyes on the flag, while reciting the Pledge of Allegiance. Afterwards, the focused 5 year olds shift their attention to the Let's Learn! wall as they now pledge their allegiance to learning. The students then say, "I will be respectful, responsible, and ready." Next they cheer "Let's Learn!" as they throw their hands up and shake their fingers with enthusiasm. This chant ignites the day's passion for learning. Last, students are encouraged to recite the daily skills posted on the Let's Learn! wall. It is certainly evident that these kindergartners are now filled with curiosity and eagerness to partake in a day bursting with adventure and excitement. They are ready to embark on their learning journey.

LET'S LEARN!

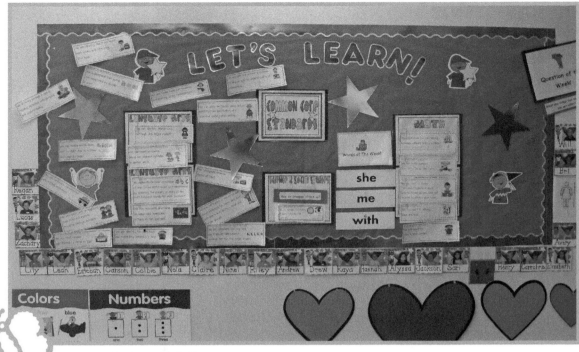

Let's Learn! Wall

Display

The first Common Core 3 routine to establish is the art of display. Display is effective in eliminating verbal miscommunication by providing needed picture prompts for young learners. An example of display in the kindergarten classroom is a Let's Learn! wall. A learning wall can serve as a visual anchor for students to rely on when articulating daily learning targets.

When creating an effective learning wall, first establish a prominent place in your classroom. Next, put each student's picture around the border of the wall to inspire ownership, interest, and a community of Common Core-focused learners. Title it "Let's Learn!" and put colorful stars all over the board to ignite excitement. Then, divide the wall into 6 separate areas for displaying each strand of the ELA standards. (RL, RI, RF, W, SL, and L) Keep paper clips permanently attached to the learning wall so the kid-friendly standards can simply be slid into the correct skill area on the day they are being targeted. You must carefully and decisively choose which standards need to be displayed to best reflect the day's learning targets. Some standards can be stapled into the wall permanently as they are integrated into all lessons daily. For example, the Speaking and Listening standards SL.K.1a–b, which involve engaging students in collaborative conversations, could be displayed on your learning wall for the entire year. Be sure to refer to this wall daily so that children internalize the importance of the Common Core and become focused learners.

A learning wall will command attention from everyone who enters your classroom. It will be evident that you are a community of Common Core-focused learners.

It is also important to display the standards at your centers. At first glance, the work at a center can appear to mimic only play. However, much academic learning is accomplished through strategic play at centers. Displaying a standard can heighten the awareness of children as well as parents and administrators who view students working in small groups.

It is essential that when you model each center you also bring attention to the aligned Common Core Standard. This can be accomplished by simply stating, "Students, what skill are we practicing at our center today?" Then encourage your students to recite the kid-friendly standard. This simple strategy can make quite a difference. Children no longer think that centers are only for playing. Instead they are active, engaged learners who can proudly articulate the standard they are practicing as they play.

Apple Roll and Read www.canyoureadityeswecan.com

Communicate

The second Common Core 3 routine is to communicate. Talk with parents about the Common Core Standards. Families play such a vital role in each child's education. It is essential to help parents become familiar with the language of the standards and use it at home with their children. This work bridges the gap between school and home. One way to achieve this goal is to have a parent Common Core night. Invite parents to school before the start of kindergarten to help foster a relationship focused on mutual goals and understanding. The purpose of this event is to introduce background information about the Common Core Standards and to make parents aware of the developmental learning domains. When parents help kindergartners develop self-help, fine motor, gross motor, and social/emotional skills prior to school, it allows for more instructional time to be spent on academics in the classroom.

Another effective way to communicate the Common Core to parents is through weekly or monthly newsletters. Instead of distributing a complete list of the Common Core Standards it is much more effective to include snippets of those that align to your classroom's current activities. These snippets should be written in kid-friendly language so that they are free from extra technical language that can overwhelm parents. This tactic brings relevance and purpose to the Common Core. Give the Common Core section of your newsletter an interesting title, such as "Hot Topics" or "Superstar Skills." Your Common Core section of your newsletter will now jump off the page, capturing the attention of parents.

It is also helpful to add kid-friendly standards to take-home activities and games. Putting a standard in the corner of a parent direction page connects powerful practice to the standard. Standards-focused parents are powerful partners because they are committed to their child's academic success. Parents who correlate standards and activities are able to cement learning at home to the Common Core Standards.

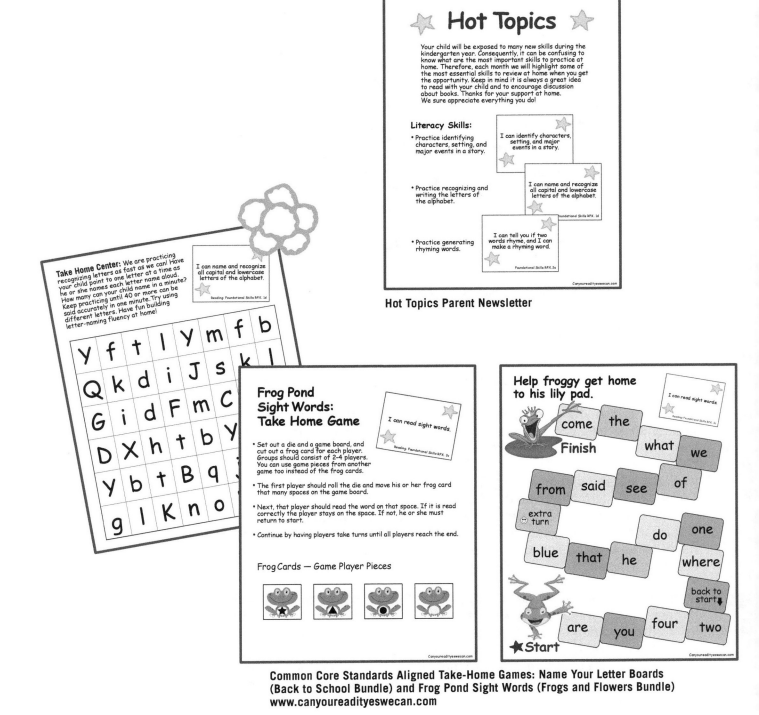

Hot Topics Parent Newsletter

Common Core Standards Aligned Take-Home Games: Name Your Letter Boards (Back to School Bundle) and Frog Pond Sight Words (Frogs and Flowers Bundle)
www.canyoureadityeswecan.com

Integrate

The last Common Core 3 routine is integration. Integrated instruction is a trademark of best practice. NAEYC (2009) advises educators not to teach young children in a fragmented manner. They specifically state this in their position statement, "Standards overload is overwhelming to teachers and children alike and can lead to potentially problematic teaching practices. At the preschool and K–3 levels particularly, practices of concern include excessive lecturing to the whole group, fragmented teaching of discreet objectives, and insistence that teachers follow rigid, tightly paced schedules."

Kindergartners lack prior knowledge and have short attention spans; therefore, integration is essential. Exposing students to multiple ELA Common Core Standards must be done daily across all content areas and instructional settings, such as science, math, social studies, and so on. Students will also gain a deeper understanding of the Common Core Standards when you engage them in opportunities to authentically apply the standards in multiple ways during small group, whole group, center play, and partner activities.

Intentional Integration

During science whole group time, I facilitated discussion about living things. Then, we talked about how good learners can remember important information by creating learning webs. As a group, we constructed a class anchor chart with living things as the topic in the center and important related facts on each hook. I intentionally integrated ELA skills, such as letter recognition, sound correspondence, writing conventions, and sight word recognition. I repeatedly referenced kid-friendly standards on the learning wall in an effort to connect science and literacy. To my amazement, Abby and Jessica independently chose to authentically apply this strategy in a cooperative learning group during writing center time. They could have written about anything. Impressively, they were eager to show me that they could be superstar science learners. This is integration at its best!

These kindergartners proudly share their student-created, science inspired learning webs.

Remember the following metaphor as you search for a map to guide you through implementing the Common Core. If learning is a journey, then the Common Core is merely an itinerary that designates desired destinations students must stop at along the way. Design differentiated road maps to guide each student in arriving at every location safely and filled with enthusiasm to continue their exploration. Plot intentional paths that encourage children to develop independence and passion at each twist and turn. Only then can you truly navigate a voyage that steers each student down the path to empowered learning.

This book is filled with routines to help you integrate and teach the rich skills supported by the standards. We've provided mini-lessons within each strand, which can be adapted to go along with the books and content areas you are teaching.

Aha Moments: Snippets for Reflection

★ The power of routines should never be underestimated.

★ Without routines we would never be able to achieve the rigorous academic skills of the Common Core Standards.

★ Children lack prior knowledge. They thrive on routines from the day they are born.

★ A daily schedule can help relieve anxiety.

★ The ultimate goal is for students to independently refer to the schedule as questions arise during their day.

★ Chanting can equate to a recipe for success in motivating student behavior.

★ Children and parents instantly develop trust in teachers when they can envision a clear picture of the kindergarten routine.

★ Consistent routines that are implemented during daily classroom work support a sense of safety, assurance, and trust in all stakeholders.

★ The Common Core 3 routines are display, communicate, and integrate.

★ Display is effective in eliminating verbal miscommunication by providing needed picture prompts for young learners.

★ A learning wall will command attention from everyone who enters your classroom. It will be clearly evident, to all that enter through your door, that you are a community of Common Core-focused learners.

★ A display of standards can heighten the awareness of children as well as parents and administrators who view students working in small groups as only play.

★ Parents who are prepared to speak Common Core language can help the bridge the gap between school and home.

★ Parents who help kindergartners develop self-help, fine motor, gross motor, and social/emotional skills prior to school allow for more instructional time to be spent on academics in the classroom.

★ Standards-focused parents are powerful partners because they are committed to their child's academic success.

★ Integrated instruction is a trademark of best practice.

★ Students must be exposed to multiple Common Core Standards daily across all content areas and instructional settings.

★ Students will gain a deeper understanding of the Common Core when they have opportunities to authentically apply the standards in multiple ways during small group, whole group, center play, and partner activities.

CHAPTER 4

WHO'S A GOOD READER? Strategies for Teaching Reading Literature (RL.K)

Children come to school naturally talking about and enjoying listening to stories. Even though their deepest desire is to read, very few kindergartners enter school with that skill.

IRA and NAEYC (1998) call for intentional emergent literacy instruction in their Joint Position Statement. "The ability to read and write does not develop naturally, without careful planning and instruction. Children need regular and active interactions with print." To successfully instruct the Reading Literature strand, you must intentionally plan for instruction. What you do before, during, and after read-alouds determines whether students will achieve their desire to walk down the path to reading.

Bundling the Standards: Reading Literature

You and your students will fail to reap the benefits of Common Core-aligned instruction if you attempt to teach the standards in an isolated, fragmented manner. You must unlock the interconnectedness of the Common Core Standards to successfully streamline instruction. The standards are meant to complement one another in an effort to provide opportunities for scaffolding higher-level thinking. For example, RL.K.3 states, "With prompting and support, identify characters, setting, and major events in a story." Students are merely expected to identify story elements on a knowledge level. Standard RL.K.9 states, "With prompting and support, compare and contrast the adventures and experiences of characters in familiar stories." This is the perfect partner standard for RL.K.3. Students are now stretched to apply their rote knowledge about characters by demonstrating higher-level thinking, such as explaining, comparing, and contrasting. Teaching these standards in tandem helps build the skills students need to become good readers. Bundling the standards will help students see that they need to use a variety of strategies to be good readers. Teaching one standard at a time could limit student-learning opportunities.

Set the stage for standards learning. Begin each lesson by referring to the Let's Learn! wall. Then, say, "Kindergartners, look at the skills we are going to practice today." Instill focus and enthusiasm for reading by having your students recite the day's posted learning targets. Continue with, "Why do you think we need to learn these skills?" Encourage students to respond with, "Because that is what good readers need to do." Cement the commitment of the class to reading by excitedly asking, "Who's a good reader?" Pump them up to respond with, "I'm a good reader!" Last, confirm their pledge by saying, "Yes you are all good readers. I am so proud of you. Now, let's learn."

Read-alouds are a fantastic strategy for teaching multiple standards within one lesson. IRA and NAEYC (1998) remind us that reading aloud to children is one of the single most important activities for building the understandings and skills necessary for reading success. The dialogue that happens before, during, and after read-alouds is essential in empowering students to make meaning from text.

Use your favorite read-alouds to facilitate collaborative conversations and encourage comprehension growth. The mini-lessons on the next few pages show you how to do it.

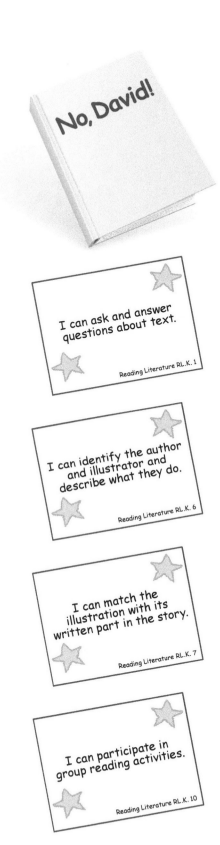

I can ask and answer questions about text.

Reading Literature RL.K.1

I can identify the author and illustrator and describe what they do.

Reading Literature RL.K.6

I can match the illustration with its written part in the story.

Reading Literature RL.K.7

I can participate in group reading activities.

Reading Literature RL.K.10

Intentionally plan for incorporating multiple standards into a lesson. In Lesson 1, the technique of questioning is used to bundle standards RL.K.1, RL.K.6, RL.K.7, and RL.K.10.

Lesson 1

No, David! by David Shannon

Published by The Blue Sky Press

It is the first day of school. You need a great read-aloud to use as a springboard to help your kindergartners understand what good readers do and how to follow rules at school.

Before reading, set the purpose for learning. Be sure to refer to the targeted standards on the Let's Learn! wall. Now that students are prepared for learning, gather children on the carpet and begin your lesson on *No, David!*

Display the front cover of the book and say, *Boys and girls, the title of this book is* No, David! *The author is David Shannon. Do you know what a title is?* Wait for appropriate responses to be shared and affirm that a title is the name of a story. Next, point to the title and say, *Let's all read the title together. Wow! I am so proud of you. You now know what a title is. Do you know what an author is and what he or she does?* Wait for appropriate responses to be shared and affirm that an author is the person who writes the story. *Have you ever written a story? If you have, you are already an author too. David Shannon is the author of this book. Let's read the author's name when I point to it.* Point to the author's name as the class reads it with you. *You are already showing me that you all are superstar readers because you know the title and author of our book today. Give yourselves a cowboy. Yeehaw!*

Do you know what else good readers do? They ask lots of questions before they read a book, while they read the book, and even after they read the book. Asking questions helps readers learn new things. I have a song that will help us remember to ask questions when we read. Using Figure 4.1,

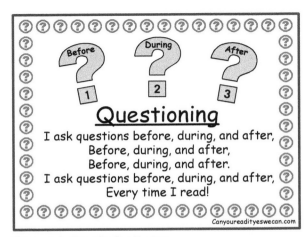

Figure 4.1: Questioning Poster
Comprehension Bundle www.canyoureadityeswecan.com

have students echo sing multiple times to the tune of "Mary Had a Little Lamb" until they can independently use the song as an anchor for learning. Hang this poster in the classroom.

Let's practice questioning. Kindergartners, look at the front cover. Let's think of some questions about the book. When I look at the front cover I wonder where is David located. Raise your hand if you are wondering something too. Discuss student responses. *That's great! I really like how all of your questions are different. Good readers pay careful attention and look for clues during the story to try to answer their questions.* To ignite curiosity whisper, *Let's be good readers and open up the book to start our reading adventure.*

Turn to the title page. *Look, this is called a title page. A title page tells us the title and the author's name too. Remember, the title is what the book is called and an author is the name of the person who wrote the story. Since you are all experts on titles and authors, we are ready to read this title page. I'll be the pointer, you be the readers.* Pause for student reading as you point to the text. *That was so awesome! Look at all of you being readers on the first day of kindergarten! Isn't reading so much fun! Give yourselves another cowboy!*

Did you remember that good readers don't just read the words? They also have to ask questions. Look at this title page. Are you wondering anything? Raise your hand if you want to share your question with the group. Help students notice the woman in the background. *I am so proud of you for noticing the illustration. Illustrations are the pictures in the book. Illustrations give us important clues about the story. I like how you were wondering if the lady in the illustration is David's mom or David's teacher. I was wondering if she was dancing, because I see her hands are on her hips and she is tapping her foot. Let's read and use the illustrations and words on each page to help us ask and answer questions.*

Turn the page. Read the text and pause for the students to be able to examine the illustration. *Raise your hand if you think that this page has helped us answer any of our questions.* Children will most likely share that the lady on the title page is David's mom. Be sure to push students to explain their thinking. *Becky, you're right! It is David's mom that we saw on the title page. How did you know? That's right, the words told us it was David's mom. Words and illustrations work together to help us make meaning.*

Let's look at the illustration on this page. Does it make you wonder anything? Turn to a friend and share your question. Turn back and put your eyes on me after you and your friend have shared a question. Listen in and provide corrective feedback to keep students on task. Continue to follow this questioning routine as you teach each page. Be sure to layer in repetition and positive reinforcement.

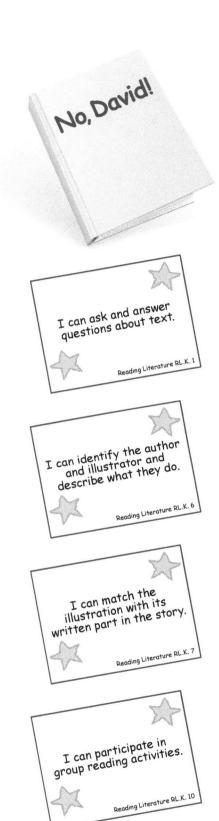

I can ask and answer questions about text.

Reading Literature RL.K.1

I can identify the author and illustrator and describe what they do.

Reading Literature RL.K.6

I can match the illustration with its written part in the story.

Reading Literature RL.K.7

I can participate in group reading activities.

Reading Literature RL.K.10

After you finish reading the book, celebrate. *Wow! You are great readers. I am so proud of the way you ask and answer questions during reading. Amazing readers ask questions when they finish reading a book too. What are you still wondering?* Wait for appropriate responses. Since it is the beginning of kindergarten, verbal responses are adequate. As the school year unfolds, be sure to scaffold instruction by recording responses on chart paper. The addition of print will provide opportunities for differentiation.

Facilitate cooperative learning by encouraging students to help one another find the answers to their questions. *Asking questions helps us understand the author's message in a book. What do you think David Shannon was trying to tell us in this book?* Accept all answers as long as students can provide evidence from the book. If students are having a difficult time responding, scaffold instruction by modeling a response. *Those are some great ideas that you have about this story. I was thinking that David Shannon, the author, wanted us to know that moms always love us even if we don't make the best choices. I think that David did a lot of naughty things, such as break a vase and write on a wall. His mom tells him "no" all the time but on the last page his mom hugs him and says she loves him.*

Guess what? Since you are such reading experts, tomorrow we're going to practice asking and answering questions before, during, and after reading with another book written by the author David Shannon. The title is David Goes to School.

On the next day, review with students how good readers use the act of questioning. Re-sing the Questioning Poster. Using *David Goes to School*, repeat the same strategies you used to teach *No, David!* Be sure to focus on using the vocabulary of the standards. Engage active participation by encouraging students to try questioning independently and with partners, and review what good readers do.

As an extension, have students make connections between the two David Shannon books and the need for having rules at school. Discuss what David would need to know about how to behave if he were a kindergartner at your school. You can even record answers on chart paper and have students illustrate the story. By engaging students in authentic writing activities after read-alouds, students will start to see the bigger picture of how to be an author and illustrator.

Center/Small Group Practice

- **Sticky Note Practice:** Have partners practice standard RL.K.1 with any text previously used in a read-aloud. Using sticky notes, ask children to indicate parts of the story where they have questions. More capable students can write the question on their sticky note using their kindergarten spelling while other students can make a question mark and stick it on the page. Be sure to give students time to share their sticky note questions with the whole class.

- **Listening Center:** Using a listening center or tablet, have students practice standards RL.K.7 and RL.K.10 with any multimedia kindergarten book that students can view. Set the purpose for learning by telling them that they will be writing about their favorite part in the book and drawing a matching illustration. Then, have students share their work. Encourage them to explain how the pictures in the book helped guide their understanding.

- **Guided Reading:** Put students in ability-level reading groups. Provide each member of your targeted group with the same appropriate leveled text. Review the strategy of questioning. Scaffold instruction as needed to engage students in practicing standards RL.K.1 and RL.K.10.

Children also need opportunity to practice what they've learned about print with their peers and on their own. (IRA and NAEYC 1998)

Independent Practice

Questioning Practice: Bring children together to model the Question Response Sheet. (See Figure 4.2.) Have students practice standards RL.K.1 and RL.K.7 with any text previously used in a read-aloud. Ask students to write about or draw questions they have before, during, and after reading. More capable students can write the questions using their kindergarten spelling while other students can draw a picture to represent their question. Last, be sure to give students time to share their questions.

TIP: Write the title of the book in the title space before you copy it for students. This allows students to focus on questioning rather than laboring over copying a title.

Parent Connections

- **Parent Night:** Model for parents how to get the most out of read-alouds at home. Show them how to help their child question and connect to text. You could also have multiple literacy nights throughout the school year to model techniques for parents.

- **Parent Newsletter:** After you have practiced a technique in the classroom multiple times, send home a comprehension newsletter. (See Figure 4.3.)

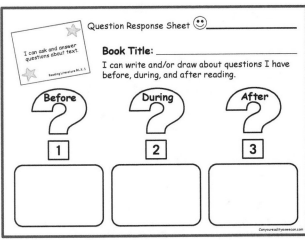

Figure 4.2
Question Response Sheet
Full page available in Appendix

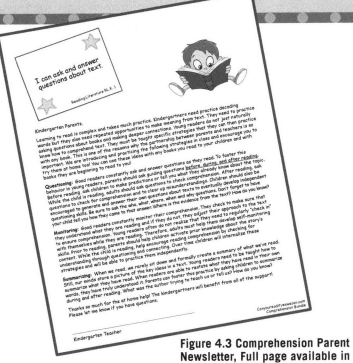

Figure 4.3 Comprehension Parent Newsletter, Full page available in Appendix

Technology Tips

- **Computer Center:** Use Internet read-aloud sites, such as Tumblebooks and Youtube, to engage students in practicing RL.K.7 and RL.K.10 with any multimedia kindergarten book. Set the purpose for learning by telling students that they will be writing about their favorite part in the story and drawing a matching illustration. Viewing stories on a computer can provide a heightened level of engagement and motivation to practice the standards. Then, have students share their work. Encourage them to explain how the pictures in the book helped guide their understanding.

- **Broadcasting Books on the Big Screen:** Use an overhead or document camera to project a book on the big screen. This will instantly engage your students, providing them a high-tech way of viewing text.

TIP: Cover the words on each page, and ask students to make predictions, ask questions, and make inferences when describing what they think will happen in the story.

Children's Books to Teach Questioning

A Big Box of Bananas by Jay Dale, published by Capstone

Believe Me, Goldilocks Rocks! by Nancy Loewen, published by Capstone

Boss of the World by Fran Manushkin, published by Capstone

Dog Breath: The Horrible Trouble with Hally Tosis by Dav Pilkey, published by The Blue Sky Press

Green Wilma by Tedd Arnold, published by Puffin

Listen, Buddy! by Helen Lester, published by HMH Books for Young Readers

Spots, Feathers, and Curly Tails by Nancy Tafuri, published by Greenwillow Books

The *Parts* series by Tedd Arnold, published by Puffin

Tops & Bottoms by Janet Stevens, published by HMH Books for Young Readers

Whistle for Willie by Ezra Jack Keats, published by Scholastic

Yo! Yes? by Chris Raschka, published by Scholastic

Reading Literature Assessment Checklist

- The ELA Assessment Checklist Reading Standards: Literature can be used while students are at play or engaged at literacy centers. (See Figures 4.4 and 4.5.)
- This tool allows for open-ended use. Sometimes you might be observing the whole class for one indicated skill. Other times you might be analyzing one child on multiple skills. You can use a check mark or a date when the skill is achieved.
- Use anecdotal records and notes while students are working independently or engaged in the classroom. You can place these notes in portfolios or digital portfolios.

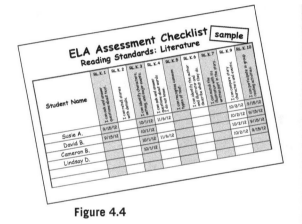

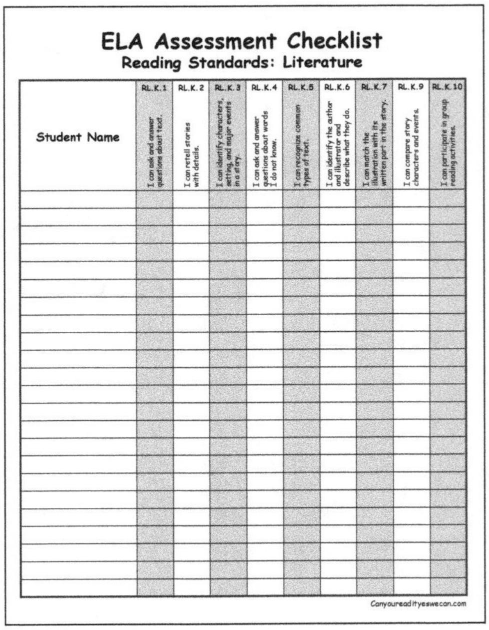

ELA Assessment Checklist sample

Reading Standards: Literature

Student Name	RL.K.1 I can ask and answer questions about text.	RL.K.2 I can retell stories with details.	RL.K.3 I can identify characters, setting, and major events.	RL.K.4 I can ask and answer questions about words I do not know.	RL.K.5 I can recognize common types of text.	RL.K.6 I can identify the author and illustrator and describe what they do.	RL.K.7 I can match the illustration with its written part in the story.	RL.K.9 I can compare story characters and events.	RL.K.10 I can participate in group reading activities.
Susie A.	9/15/12		10/1/12	11/6/12				10/2/12	9/15/12
David B.	9/15/12		10/1/12					10/2/12	9/15/12
Cameron B.			10/1/12	11/6/12				10/2/12	9/15/12
Lindsay D.			10/1/12					10/2/12	9/15/12

Figure 4.4

ELA Assessment Checklist

Reading Standards: Literature

Student Name	RL.K.1 I can ask and answer questions about text.	RL.K.2 I can retell stories with details.	RL.K.3 I can identify characters, setting, and major events in a story.	RL.K.4 I can ask and answer questions about words I do not know.	RL.K.5 I can recognize common types of text.	RL.K.6 I can identify the author and illustrator and describe what they do.	RL.K.7 I can match the illustration with its written part in the story.	RL.K.9 I can compare story characters and events.	RL.K.10 I can participate in group reading activities.

Canyoureadityeswecan.com

Figure 4.5 ELA Assessment Checklist Reading Standards: Literature Full page available in Appendix

Intentionally plan for incorporating multiple standards into a lesson. In Lesson 2, the technique of retelling plot is used to bundle standards RL.K.2, RL.K.3, RL.K.9, and RL.K.10. For this lesson we are using one of our favorite books. This lesson could be applied to any fiction book and any theme.

Lesson 2

Chicken Little
by Christianne C. Jones
Published by Capstone

Discussing the elements of a story—characters, setting, and plot—helps students comprehend a narrative text. A deeper understanding of how stories work can assist students in developing a greater appreciation of literature and a framework to guide them in writing stories of their own. Fables and folktales are the perfect text to encourage comprehension growth. The concise structure and rich language of fables help young readers recognize predictable story patterns and develop critical thinking skills. Fables challenge children to reflect on their own values and morals by making inferences and judgments.

Before reading, set the purpose for learning. Be sure to refer to the targeted standards on the Let's Learn! wall. Now that students are prepared for learning, gather children on the carpet and begin your *Chicken Little* lesson.

Display the front cover of the book and say, *Boys and girls, the title of this book is* Chicken Little. *This story is a fable and is retold by Christianne C. Jones. Fables are narrative stories. They have three important parts: characters, setting, and plot. Good readers are able to identify these three important parts when they read narratives.*

Today, we are going to practice plot. When we talk about plot, we talk about the events that happen in a story. If we think about when the events happen, it is easier to remember the plot. Encourage students to use three fingers to represent the three parts of plot.

When I talk about the plot, I always say what happens in the beginning, middle, and end of the story. Here is a song to help us learn about plot. Using the Plot Song Poster in Figure 4.6, have students echo sing to the tune of "Mary Had a Little Lamb" multiple times until they can independently use the song as an anchor for learning. Hang this poster in the classroom.

Now let's practice plot with a story. Kindergartners, does anyone remember what plot is in a story? Raise your hand if you can tell us about plot. Accept all reasonable answers.

I can retell stories with details.

Reading Literature RL.K. 2

I can identify characters, setting, and major events in a story.

Reading Literature RL.K. 3

I can compare story characters and events.

Reading Literature RL.K. 9

I can participate in group reading activities.

Reading Literature RL.K. 10

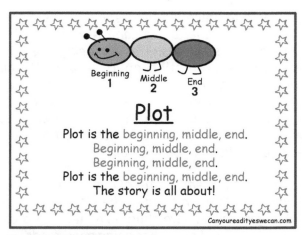

Figure 4.6 Plot Song Poster
Comprehension Bundle www.canyoureadityeswecan.com

Before reading *Chicken Little*, review the title and the author. Have students make predictions about what might happen in the story. You can record student responses on chart paper. *Wow! These are great predictions about what might happen in the story. I love how you used the illustration on the front cover to help you make predictions. Let's see if any of your predictions are in the plot of this story. Sometimes when I make predictions I guess right but many times I am wrong. Good readers keep reading and changing their predictions as the story unfolds.*

Begin reading *Chicken Little*. Stop after page 2 and discuss what happened in the beginning of the story. *Friends, let's think about what happened in the story so far. What would be a good sentence to summarize the beginning events of the story?* Accept all answers but encourage concise responses, such as: "An acorn fell on Chicken Little's head." "She thought the sky was falling and wanted to tell the king." Also, ask students to support their responses with evidence from the text by asking, *Why do you think that?* Accept student responses. *Are there any new predictions you want to add to our chart now? I am thinking that more acorns might fall on her head on her way to see the king. Let's add that to the chart. Does anyone else have a new prediction?* Add responses.

Now let's read on to find out what happens in the middle of the story. Read until Chicken Little meets Turkey Lurkey. Stop and discuss. *Class, who can tell us a good sentence that summarizes what happened in the middle of the story?* Accept all answers but encourage concise responses, such as: "She met lots of friends and asked them to go with her to talk to the king." Ask students to support their responses with evidence from the text. Praise students with a round of applause. *Are there any new predictions you want to add to our chart now?* Add responses.

Now, we are ready to see what happens at the end of the story. Read to the end and discuss events. *Wow! What an exciting ending. Who can describe what happened at the end of* Chicken Little? Accept all answers but encourage concise responses, such as: "They met a fox that tricked and ate them." Also, ask students to support their responses with evidence from the text.

Inspire students to make inferences and connections. *How do you know that the fox ate the other characters?* Also ask students to make a judgment about the fox's actions. *Was fox being a good friend? Why or why not?* Refer to the prediction chart created throughout the lesson. *Remember when we made predictions about what we thought would happen in the story of* Chicken Little? *Let's check and see if any of them were right.* Go through each response and circle correct predictions. *Look at all of our great predictions about the plot. Good readers are always making and checking predictions as they read.*

Good readers also remember the plot by thinking about what happens at the beginning, middle, and end of the story. I like to call that the Plot 3. Hold up 3 fingers as you have children recite the words beginning, middle, and end. *I am so proud of you for being good readers. Let's review the plot of* Chicken Little *by doing the Plot 3. Hold up one finger like me and say what happened at the beginning of the story. An acorn fell on Chicken Little's head. Now it is your turn.* Children repeat. *Hold up two fingers and say what happened in the middle. She met lots of friends on her way to the king. Now it is your turn.* Children repeat. *Hold up three fingers and say what happened at the end of the story. The fox tricked everyone and ate them. Now it is your turn.* Children repeat. *You are so fantastic at doing the Plot 3 that you are now ready to try it with a partner. When I say go, turn to a friend and share the Plot 3 about the story of* Chicken Little. *Turn back and put your eyes on me after you and your friend have shared the Plot 3.* Listen in and provide corrective feedback to keep students on task. Have students share responses with the class.

Wouldn't it be fun to share the Plot 3 with your parents? They would be so proud of you for knowing the plot of Chicken Little. *This Plot 3 paper will help us organize our thoughts so we can share the story. Let's create one together. Make sure you pay careful attention because you get to make one*

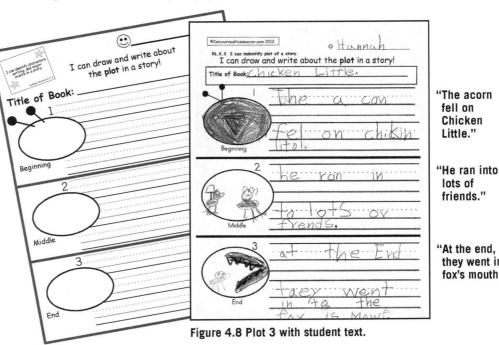

"The acorn fell on Chicken Little."

"He ran into lots of friends."

"At the end, they went into fox's mouth."

Figure 4.8 Plot 3 with student text.

Figure 4.7 Plot 3 Paper
Full page available in Appendix

later to take home. Guide students in completing the Plot 3 paper as a class first and then independently. (See Figures 4.7 and 4.8.) Be sure to share completed responses in the Author's Chair. After students have shared their Plot 3 papers, praise them for their efforts. Post the Plot 3 poster in the classroom and refer to it often as a prompt for retelling stories.

Guess what! Since you are such reading experts, tomorrow we're going to practice the Plot 3 with another fable called Henny Penny. *Then we are going to compare how the plots are the same and contrast how the plots are different.*

On the next day, review with students how good readers do the Plot 3. Re-sing the Plot Song Poster. Using *Henny Penny*, repeat the same routine used when teaching the *Chicken Little* book. Engage active participation by encouraging students to apply the skill of identifying plot with partners.

As an extension, have students compare and contrast the plots of *Chicken Little* and *Henny Penny*. You can even record answers on chart paper. You can apply this same routine when teaching the other two story elements of characters and setting. Eventually, students should be able to identify all three elements when reading narratives. Also with prompting and support, students should be able to use higher-level thinking to compare and contrast story elements between texts.

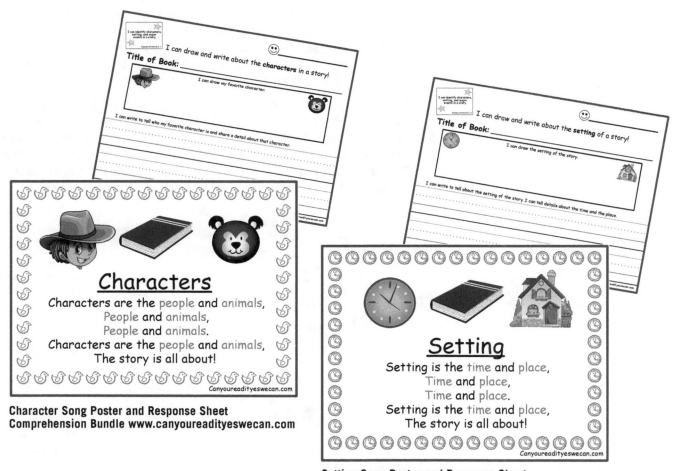

Character Song Poster and Response Sheet
Comprehension Bundle www.canyoureadityeswecan.com

Setting Song Poster and Response Sheet
Comprehension Bundle www.canyoureadityeswecan.com

Center/Small Group Practice

- **Beach Ball Practice:** Put students in a small group circle. Engage them in practicing standard RL.K.3 with any text previously used in a read-aloud. Be sure to place a copy of the book in the center of the circle to provide a visual cue. Label each colored part of a beach ball with a different story element (i.e., characters, setting, plot). Have students toss the ball to a friend in the circle. The student who catches the ball must identify the story element that his or her thumb is touching. For example, if I caught the beach ball with my thumb on character, I would have to identify a main character in the targeted book.

- **Theater Center:** Have students practice RL.K.2 by retelling the plot of a familiar story using puppets.

- **Guided Reading:** Put students in ability-level reading groups. Provide each member of your targeted group with the same appropriately leveled narrative text. Review a targeted story element. Scaffold instruction as needed to engage students in practicing standards RL.K.3 and RL.K.10. To differentiate instruction for more capable students, have them compare two texts to practice standard RL.K.9.

Independent Practice

Story Element Practice: Engage students in standards RL.K.2 and RL.K.3. After a read-aloud, ask students to write about or draw the plot using a Plot 3 graphic organizer or something similar. More capable students can write using their kindergarten spelling while other students can draw a picture to represent their response. Last, be sure to give students time to share.

TIP: Write the title of the book in the title space on the graphic organizer before you copy it for students. This lets students focus on the skill of identifying plot rather than laboring over copying a title. The same independent practice activity can be applied to character and setting. This is a great authentic assessment tool! Keep a copy in student writing folders to show growth in comprehension and writing.

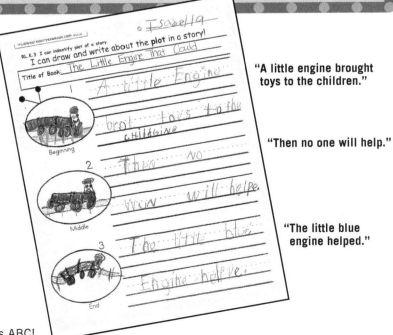

"A little engine brought toys to the children."

"Then no one will help."

"The little blue engine helped."

Parent Connections

- **Parent Night:** Model for parents how to get the most out of read-alouds at home. Show them how to help their children identify story elements. You could also have multiple literacy nights throughout the school year to introduce techniques.

- **Parent Letter:** After you have practiced story elements in the classroom multiple times, send home a parent letter, such as the Story Elements Newsletter. (See Figure 4.9.)

Figure 4.9 Story Elements Newsletter Full page available in Appendix

Technology Tips

- **Computer Center:** Use a computer or tablet to engage students in practicing standard RL.K.3 with any multimedia kindergarten book that students can view. Set the purpose for learning by telling them that they will be writing about the setting of the book and drawing a matching illustration. This could also be implemented for characters and plot.

- **Broadcasting Books on the Big Screen:** Use an overhead or document camera to project a book on the big screen. This will instantly engage your students, providing them a high-tech way of viewing text.

TIP: Cover the picture of the setting in the book. Ask students to listen carefully to the description and draw their version of the setting. Have students compare and contrast their drawings to the actual illustrations in the book. You can apply this technique to characters too.

Children's Books to Teach Story Elements

Caps for Sale: A Tale of a Peddler, Some Monkeys and Their Monkey Business by Esphyr Slobodkina, published by HarperCollins

Corduroy series by Don Freeman, published by Puffin

Fairy Tales Classroom Collection, published by Capstone

Goldilocks by Dom DeLuise, published by Aladdin

Hansel and Gretel by Dom DeLuise, published by Aladdin

If You Give a Mouse a Cookie series by Laura Joffe Numeroff, published by HarperCollins

My First Classic Story series (fables), published by Capstone

Owl Moon by Jane Yolen, published by Philomel Books

Purple, Green and Yellow by Robert Munsch, published by Annick Press

Skippyjon Jones books by Judy Schachner, published by Puffin

The Giving Tree by Shel Silverstein, published by HarperCollins

The Kissing Hand by Audrey Penn, published by Tanglewood Press

Reading Literature Assessment Checklist

- The ELA Assessment Checklist Reading Standards: Literature can be used while students are at play or engaged at literacy centers. (See Figures 4.4 and 4.5 on page 40.)

- This tool allows for open-ended use. Sometimes you might be observing the whole class for one indicated skill. Other times you might be analyzing one child on multiple skills. You can use a check mark or a date when the skill is achieved.

- Use anecdotal records and notes while students are working independently or engaged in the classroom. You can place these notes in portfolios or digital portfolios.

These kindergartners are role-playing their favorite caps as a reaction to the story *Caps for Sale: A Tale of a Peddler, Some Monkeys and Their Monkey Business.*

CHAPTER 5

WHO'S A GOOD DETECTIVE? Strategies for Teaching Informational Text (RI.K)

Kindergartners thrive on learning new facts because it helps them make sense of the world. When given the choice between reading a fiction or a nonfiction text, most young children pick nonfiction. They are drawn to the unique visual features and facts that instantly inspire connections. Informational text quenches a child's thirst for knowledge. When children are exposed to nonfiction text, they not only learn to read but they read to learn. Nonfiction is certainly a great way to engage students in rich informational text experiences that deepen vocabulary, expand schema, and strengthen critical thinking skills.

Reading informational text is meaningful and purposeful because it is practical. Think about the text that you read on your personal time. How much of it is fiction and how much is informational? Real life demands that we read newspapers, menus, directions, travel brochures, recipes, weather reports, maps, and so on. Life rarely allows us the time to read fiction.

This kindergartner is a Bubble Super Scientist!

As children grow, the amount of informational text they are required to read increases. At the fourth-grade level, children are expected to fluently read and comprehend content area textbooks with text features, including diagrams, maps, graphs, and tables. We must accept the charge of creating classrooms filled with informational text. Only then, can we prepare students for the heightened demands of content reading in the upper grades and adulthood.

The Common Core Standards call for us to use informational text more frequently. Yet, many early childhood educators are still more comfortable using fiction. Focusing only on fiction limits a child's exposure to a variety of texts and ultimately obstructs his or her literacy learning. Yopp and Yopp (2000) encourage teachers to increase student exposure to nonfiction text. "Informational texts present readers with distinctly different text structures and features than those of narrative texts. Primary-grade students must build an understanding of the conventions of informational text and develop comprehension strategies to assist learning." We must increase student exposure to informational text so that our students can absorb all the benefits of its distinct structure.

Can You Find the Evidence? Yes We Can!

Too often we limit using informational text in the classroom because we think the content is too difficult for our students to comprehend. Don't let informational text instruction intimidate you. Informational text should be viewed as a catalyst for learning instead of a mountain that cannot be climbed. Young learners are empowered by informational text if the approach is developmentally appropriate. Why not ask students to role-play a fact-finding detective? When encouraged to "switch on their searchlights," young children are instantly engaged.

Kindergartners enjoy interacting with one another while being challenged with the task of finding information during nonfiction read-alouds. The cooperative nature of becoming a classroom of detectives, all on the same mission, creates a focused learning community. The collaborative conversations further enhance comprehension by providing students the opportunity to learn from one another.

Don't just stop instruction at the knowledge level. When a student answers a question, be sure to ask, "Why do you think that? Where is the evidence?" Having kindergartners back up their responses with text evidence engages them in higher-level thinking, such as analyzing, summarizing, and supporting. Create a classroom of kindergartners that are excited to "switch on their searchlights" and learn new information. When you say, "Can you find the evidence?" they will enthusiastically say, "Yes we can!"

Set the stage for standards learning. Begin each lesson by referring to the Let's Learn! wall and saying, "Kindergartners, look at the skills we are going to practice today." Instill focus and enthusiasm for reading by having your students recite the day's posted learning targets. Continue with, "Why do you think we need to learn these skills?" Encourage students to respond with, "Because that is what good readers need to do." Cement the commitment of the class to reading informational text by excitedly asking, "Who's a good detective?" Pump them up to respond "I'm a good detective!" Last, confirm their pledge by saying, "Yes, you are good detectives. I am so proud of you. Now, let's learn."

Classroom artwork shows facts from texts.

I can identify the main idea and give details of the text.

Reading Informational RI.K.2

I can identify the front cover, back cover, and title page of a book.

Reading Informational RI.K.5

I can identify the author and illustrator and describe what they do.

Reading Informational RI.K.6

I can match the illustration with its written part in the story.

Reading Informational RI.K.7

I can find evidence in a text to support the author's main idea.

Reading Informational RI.K.8

I can participate in group reading activities.

Reading Informational RI.K.10

You should intentionally plan for incorporating multiple standards into a lesson. In Lesson 1, the technique of identifying main idea and details is used to bundle standards RI.K.2, RI.K.5, RI.K.6, RI.K.7, RI.K.8, and RI.K.10. Also, since reading, foundational skills, writing, speaking, and listening are mutually reinforcing skills, several of these strand areas are naturally integrated in the lesson.

Lesson 1

True or False? Weather by Daniel Nunn

Published by Capstone

This lesson uses one of our favorite books written about the theme of weather. This lesson could be applied to any nonfiction book and any theme.

Prior to Lesson 1, help students understand the difference between fiction and nonfiction text by reminding them of a time when you have read a fictional story about weather. A great book to refer to is *Cloudy with a Chance of Meatballs. Class, today we are going to practice reading an informational text about weather. Informational texts are different from fictional stories that have characters, setting, and plot. The author of a fictional book writes the story to entertain us. Remember the story,* Cloudy with a Chance of Meatballs? *It was a pretend adventure about food falling from the sky during all different types of weather. Could this really happen? No, that is why it is called fiction. The author wrote it to have fun and entertain us. Today, we are going to read a new type of book that is filled with information. The author wrote it to make our brains smarter about weather. We can call this type of informational book a nonfiction book. Nonfiction books are special because they help us learn new things.*

Gather children on the carpet and begin your *True or False? Weather* lesson. Display the front cover of the book and say, *Boys and girls, the title of this book is* True or False? Weather. *Do you remember what a title is?* Wait for appropriate responses to be shared and affirm that a title is the name of a book. *This is an informational book, so the title is really important because it gives us a clue as to what the author wants us to learn. Let's read the title together and see if we can figure out what the author wants us to learn today.* Point to the title and read it together as a class. *What do you think we will be learning?* Pause for students to share responses. Encourage students to use the front cover illustration as a clue. Confirm that you will be learning about the weather. *Before we read about weather, let's figure out who the author of this book is. Do you remember what an author does?* Wait for appropriate responses to be shared and affirm that an author is the person who writes the book. *The author of this book is Daniel Nunn.* Ask students to repeat the name of the author. *Wow! I am so proud of you. You are already showing me that you all are superstar readers because you know the title and author of our book today. Give yourselves a cowboy. Yeehaw!*

When good readers read informational text, they remember the main idea and important details. The main idea is the one big idea of the book. The main idea is the glue that connects all of the other parts together. The details are the parts of the book that give us examples of the main idea. I have a song that will help us understand what the main idea and important details are. Display the Main Idea Song Poster (Figure 5.1) at the easel. Have students echo sing multiple times to the tune of "Bingo" until they can independently use the song as an anchor for learning. Review what the terms "main idea" and "details" mean.

Figure 5.1. Main Idea Song Poster
Reading Informational Bundle www.canyoureadityeswecan.com

Hang the Main Idea Song Poster in the classroom. Create some short verbal practice passages and guide students in applying the concepts of main idea and details. (See Figure 5.2.)

Verbal Practice Passage

School is great. We learn at school. We read books at school. We play with friends at school.

Main Idea: School is great.

Supporting details: We learn, we read books, we play with friends.

Figure 5.2 Verbal Practice Passage

Now let's practice finding the main idea and details in our special weather book. Turn on your searchlights. Have students make a switching on gesture. *Get your brains ready to be detectives that look for clues.* Display the front cover of the book and reread the title. Read the title page next. Pause and discuss the Table of Contents. *Look at this page. It is called a Table of Contents. A Table of Contents tells us where we can find important information in the book. Good readers always read this part of the book carefully to get their brains ready for the book. Reading the Table of Contents is like getting a preview of what is inside.* Display and read this page. *Wow! Now we know more about what this book is going to be about. We are ready to read the pages. Remember to think about the main idea and details as we read.*

I can identify the main idea and give details of the text.

Reading Informational RI.K.2

I can identify the front cover, back cover, and title page of a book.

Reading Informational RI.K.5

I can identify the author and illustrator and describe what they do.

Reading Informational RI.K.6

I can match the illustration with its written part in the story.

Reading Informational RI.K.7

I can find evidence in a text to support the author's main idea.

Reading Informational RI.K.8

I can participate in group reading activities.

Reading Informational RI.K.10

Read page 4. *"The Weather* (heading) *There are lots of different types of weather. How much do you know about the weather?"* Discuss the illustrations and how they support the text by representing sunny, rainy, snowy, and windy weather. Activate prior knowledge and have students share what they already know about the weather. Praise students. *Fantastic! You already know so much about weather. That is awesome. Good readers can always learn something new too! What do you think the main idea of this book is? How do you know?* Affirm that the main idea is weather. *Yes, the main idea of this book is weather. The glue that connects all of the pages is weather. That means on each page the author will share a different weather detail. Let's read all of the pages and be weather detail detectives. Who's a good detective?* Students should chant, "I'm a good detective!"

Read page 5. *"What to Wear* (heading) *We wear coats, hats, and scarves when the weather is hot and sunny. True or False?"* Stop and discuss this statement. Have students evaluate if they think this statement is true or false and explain why. You can have students show a thumbs-up for true and a thumbs-down for false. You can also use a turn and talk and have students share with a partner or have students share in whole group. *I like how you are able to tell me why you think this statement is false. Let's turn the page and see if your prediction is right.*

Read page 6. *"False!* (heading) *We wear coats, hats, and scarves when the weather is cold. The clothes keep us warm!"* Stop and discuss. *Yes you were right! This statement was false. I really like the way the author asks us to predict if the statement is true or false. It makes the book fun to read and helps us learn about weather too! Let's keep reading for more details about weather and keep being detectives.* Continue the same reading routine. Be sure to encourage collaborative conversations and higher-level thinking by asking students to explain the evidence behind their responses.

After finishing the book, review the main idea and supporting details. *This book is a nonfiction book. The author wrote it to help us learn information. Good readers of informational text can identify the main idea and tell about the details too. Who can raise their hand and share the main idea of this book?* Accept all answers but encourage concise responses. Provide corrective feedback if they give a detail instead. Have students state the main idea together. *You are so smart! The main idea of this book is weather. The author shares information about weather on each page. Weather is the glue that holds this book together.*

Remembering the details can be much more challenging because there are so many of them. I usually have to read an informational book many times so that I can remember the details. Let's read the book again, but this time let's play the Grab It Game when we read. To play this game, you will need to reach out and quietly grab the details as I read. Model stretching out your hand and grabbing the air. This kinesthetic strategy will actively engage students as you read and provide a prompt for remembering details.

Read the entire book again. Pause and guide students to grab the details as you read. *I really like the way you grabbed the details. Give yourselves some fireworks for being such awesome detectives for details. Good readers don't just sit and listen. They are always thinking about the words and work hard to remember the details. What details did you grab? When I say go, turn to a friend and share two details that you grabbed. When you are done sharing, turn to the front and put your hands in your lap. Go!* Have students turn and talk with a friend about the details in the book. Provide corrective feedback and scaffolding as needed. Have students share responses with the whole group. *You are fantastic informational readers! You can identify the main idea and the key details when you read. Awesome job!*

Your parents would be so proud of you if you shared what we learned today with them at home. You can show them by writing about the main idea and details on this very special paper. (See Figure 5.3.)

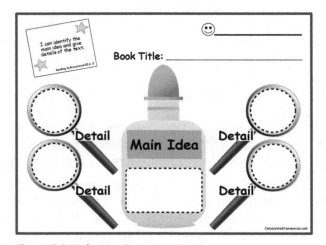 

Figure 5.3 Main Idea Response Sheet
Full page available in Appendix

Engage students in a shared writing lesson. *I already wrote the title on the title line. You will need to write your name by the happy face. What do you think we will need to write about here on the glue bottle?* Affirm that this is where we write "weather" because weather was the main idea of the book. *Yes, since the main idea is the glue that holds the story together, we need to write the main idea on the glue bottle.* Model writing the word "weather." Encourage students to use their kindergarten spelling or draw pictures to represent their words.

Now look at the magnifying glasses. Who uses a magnifying glass? Yes, a detective uses a magnifying glass. We were detectives for details about weather. We need to write a detail on each magnifier. Have students share details and model write them in the appropriate places.

Nice job! This special paper shows what we remember about the main idea and details in the book, True or False? Weather. *Your families are going to be so proud of you when you bring home one of these special papers. Now it is time for you to write your own.* Send students to their seats to complete a main idea response sheet independently. Provide scaffolding as needed.

Center/Small Group Practice

- **Weather Forecast Calendar Center:** Put blank monthly calendars at a center. Set out several nonfiction weather books to use as references. Remind students that you have been practicing the main idea of a weather book and different types of weather as details about the topic. Engage students in practicing standard RI.K.2 and RI.K.7 using the books. Then, ask children to predict what the weather will be like for the current month. Have students write or draw their weather word on each day. More capable students can write weather words using their kindergarten spelling while other students can just draw a picture. Last, be sure to give students time to share their weather predictions. It will be fun for children to display their calendars and check them each day.

- **True or False Bucket:** Set out several weather nonfiction books. Write down sentences about weather on small strips that could be checked by using the books. Be sure to make some true and some false. Put them in a bucket. Group students in partners or small groups to play. Engage students in practicing standard RI.K.2 using the books. Then have them practice RI.K.8. One student takes out sentence strip and reads it. The other student guesses if it is true or false. Then together they look for evidence in a book to support their response. You might want to have a parent volunteer help with reading the sentence strips.

- **Main Idea Sort:** Engage students in practicing standard RI.K.2 by having them sort real objects or pictures. Put several items in a basket that have to do with the book you are studying. Include several items that do not belong. Kindergartners should sort them into two groups (for example, "Weather" and "Not Weather"). Students could label the groups and objects too!

- **Guided Reading:** Put students in ability-level reading groups. Provide each member of your targeted group with the same appropriate leveled nonfiction text. Review finding the main idea and supporting details. Scaffold instruction as needed to engage students in practicing standards RI.K.2, RI.K.8, and RI.K.10.

Independent Practice

Main Idea Practice: Bring students together to model the Main Idea Response Sheet. (See Figure 5.3 on page 55.) Engage students in practicing standards RI.K.2 and RI.K.8 with any nonfiction text previously used in a read-aloud. Ask students to write about or draw the main idea and details using this graphic organizer. More capable students can write responses using their kindergarten spelling while other students can draw a picture. Last, be sure to give students time to share their responses.

TIP: Write the title of the book in the title space before you copy for students. This allows students to focus on comprehension rather than laboring over copying a title.

Parent Connections

• **Parent Night:** Share with parents how important it is to read and discuss informational text at home. Model how to encourage children to find the main idea and details.

• **Parent Letter:** After you have practiced identifying the main idea and details in the classroom multiple times, send home an Informational Text Newsletter. (See Figure 5.4.)

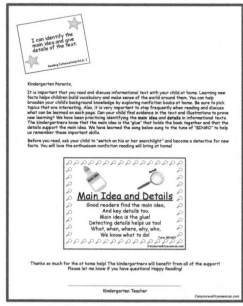

Figure 5.4 Informational Text Newsletter
Full page available in the Appendix

Technology Tips

- **Computer Center:** Use Internet read-aloud sites, such as Tumblebooks and Youtube, to engage students in practicing RI.K.2, RI.K.8, and RI.K.10 with any multimedia kindergarten book that students can view. Set the purpose for learning by telling students that they will be writing about main idea and details. Viewing stories on a computer can provide a heightened level of engagement and motivation to practice the standards. Have students complete a Main Idea Response Sheet when done listening to story.

- **Create a Multimedia Slide Show:** Using Kidspiration, PowerPoint, or Kid Pix, engage students in practicing RI.K.2. Have each student make a page and then join them all together in a show! You can set up a template, possibly in the shape of a web, so that kindergartners just have to add in words and illustrate. They will love watching it over and over again!

Children's Books to Teach Main Idea and Details

The lesson just discussed focused on the theme of weather, so we have included several of our favorite weather books below. Remember, you can use any nonfiction theme to practice the Reading Informational Text Standards.

A Cloudy Day by Melvin and Gilda Berger, published by Scholastic

A Sunny Day by Melvin and Gilda Berger, published by Scholastic

A Windy Day by Melvion and Gilda Berger, published by Scholastic

Down Comes the Rain by Franklyn M. Branley, published by HarperCollins

Eyewitness Explorers: Weather by J. Farndon, published by DK Children

Forecasting Weather by Terri Sievert, published by Capstone

Pebble Plus: Weather Basics by Erin Edison, published by Capstone

Rain and Hail by Franklyn M. Branley, published by Thomas Y. Crowell

Weather Watchers set, published by Capstone

What Will the Weather Be Like Today? by Paul Rogers, published by Scholastic

Reading Informational Assessment Checklist

- The ELA Assessment Checklist Reading Standards: Informational Text can be used while students are at play or engaged at literacy centers. (See Figures 5.5 and 5.6.)

- This tool allows for open-ended use. Sometimes you might be observing the whole class for one indicated skill. Other times you might be analyzing one child on multiple skills. You can use a check mark or a date when the skill is achieved.

- Use anecdotal records and notes while students are working independently or engaged in the classroom. You can place these notes in portfolios or digital portfolios.

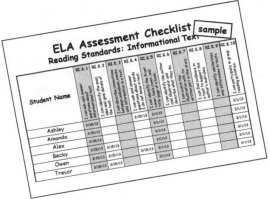

Figure 5.5

ELA Assessment Checklist
Reading Standards: Informational Text

Student Name	RI.K.1	RI.K.2	RI.K.3	RI.K.4	RI.K.5	RI.K.6	RI.K.7	RI.K.8	RI.K.9	RI.K.10
	I can ask and answer questions about informational text.	I can identify the main idea and give details of the text.	I can describe connections between individuals, events, and information in a text.	I can ask and answer questions about words I do not know in text.	I can identify the front cover, back cover, and title page of a book.	I can identify the author and illustrator and describe what they do.	I can match the illustration with its written part in the story.	I can find evidence in a text to support the author's main idea.	I can identify similarities and differences in texts.	I can participate in group reading activities.

Canyoureadityeswecan.com

Figure 5.6
ELA Assessment Checklist Reading Standards:
Informational Text
Full page available in Appendix

Prior to Lesson 2, be sure to have students review the following targets on the Let's Learn! wall so that they are focused on the essential skills of the lesson: Standards RI.K.1, RI.K.4, RI.K.5, RI.K.6, and RI.K.10. Also, since reading, foundational skills, writing, speaking, and listening are mutually reinforcing skills, several of these strand areas are naturally integrated in the lesson.

Lesson 2

Fun at the Zoo by Molly Dise

Published by Capstone from Wonder Readers Complete Package

This lesson includes one of our favorite informational books written about the zoo. It could be applied to any nonfiction book and any theme.

Help students understand the difference between fiction and nonfiction text by reminding them of a time when you have read a fiction story about zoos. A great book to refer to is *The Underpants Zoo. Class, today we are going to practice reading an informational text about zoos. Informational texts are different than fictional stories that have characters, setting, and plot. The author of a fictional book writes the story to entertain us. Remember the story,* The Underpants Zoo? *It was a pretend adventure with silly animal characters. Could this really happen? No, that is why it is called a fictional story. The author wrote it just to have fun and entertain us. Today, we are going to read a new type of book that is filled with information. The author wrote it to make our brains smarter about zoos. We can call this type of informational book a nonfiction book. Nonfiction books are special because they help us learn new things. Let's get our brains ready to learn today!*

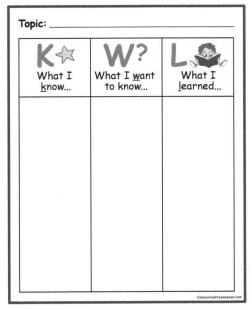

Figure 5.7 KWL Class Chart
Full page available in Appendix

Gather children on the carpet to begin the *Fun at the Zoo* lesson. *Today we are going to learn how to be good readers by asking and answering questions about information in books. We are going to use this special paper to help us organize our thoughts.* (See Figure 5.7.) *This paper is called a KWL Chart.* Point to the chart and explain what type of information you will be putting in each column.

We are going to use this KWL Chart today as we read a new book. Display the front cover of the book and say, *Boys and girls, the title of this book is* Fun at the Zoo. *Do you remember what a title is?* Wait for appropriate responses to be shared and affirm that a title is the name of a book. *This is an informational book, so the title is really important because it gives us a clue on what the author wants us to learn. Let's read the title together and see if we can figure out what the author wants us to learn today.* Point to the title and read it together as a class. *What do you think we will be learning?* Pause for students to share responses. Encourage students to use the front cover illustration as a clue. Confirm that you will be learning about the zoo. *Yes, our topic is zoos, so on our KWL Chart I am going to write "Zoo" on the topic line.*

Great readers think about what they already know about a topic before they read. This helps them make connections to the story and understand the book better. Who can share what you already know about the zoo? Accept all responses. *Wow, you know so much about the zoo. Let's use our KWL Chart to help us organize our thoughts. Right here is the K column on the chart. This is where we write what we already **know** about a topic.* Write in the student responses.

I am always curious and I really like to learn new things. Can you think of something new that you would like to know about the zoo? Great readers ask questions. What questions do you have about the zoo? Encourage students to look at the front cover to help them generate ideas. Accept all responses. *Let's use our KWL Chart again to help us organize our thoughts. Right here is the W column. This is where we write what we **want** to learn about our topic.* Write in student questions. *You are great thinkers. Give yourselves a round of applause. I can't wait to find out the answers to your questions.*

Now we are ready to read. Display the front cover of the book and reread the title. Next, read the title page, which also includes a Table of Contents. Pause and discuss the Table of Contents. *Look at this part. It is called a Table of Contents. A Table of Contents tells us where we can find important information in the book. Good readers always read this part of the book carefully to get their brains ready for the book. Reading the Table of Contents is like getting a preview of what is inside.*

Display and read this page. *Wow! Now we know what this book is going to be about. We are ready to read the pages. Remember to be thinking in your brain about our KWL Chart and look for answers to our questions.*

I can ask and answer questions about informational text.

Reading Informational RI.K. 1

I can ask and answer questions about words I do not know in text.

Reading Informational RI.K. 4

I can identify the front cover, back cover, and title page of a book.

Reading Informational RI.K. 5

I can identify the author and illustrator and describe what they do.

Reading Informational RI.K. 6

I can participate in group reading activities.

Reading Informational RI.K. 10

Read pages 2–5. Pause to discuss new vocabulary. *Kindergartners, this book tells us that some animals at the zoo are endangered. "Endangered" could be a new word for us. Does anyone know what it means?* Pause for responses. *Since we don't know what endangered means we need to add a question right here on our KWL Chart.* Point to the W column on your chart. Write in, "What is endangered?" *Good readers are always asking new questions as they read. I am so excited to learn a new word with you. Let's see if the author teaches us what endangered means. Detectives switch on your searchlights and listen for clues in the next sentence.* Read to the end of the paragraph and then discuss the definition of endangered. Encourage students to give an example of an endangered animal. *Look, we just learned what endangered means! Let's write our new information in the L column for learned on our KWL Chart.* Write the definition of endangered on chart. *Wow, it's exciting to learn new words. Informational books make us so smart! Let's keep reading to see what else we can learn about the zoo!*

Continue this routine with each section of the text. Be sure to encourage students to ask and answer questions using the KWL format. Update the class KWL Chart as you read. Draw attention to new vocabulary and illustrations. Discuss the use of photos to convey meaning. *Detectives, did you notice anything about the illustrations in this book?* Flip through several illustrations so that students can make comparisons. Pause and accept all answers. Encourage students to notice that real photographs are used in this book. *Why do you think the book doesn't include a cartoon picture of a monkey or a dolphin?* Pause for responses. Assist children in understanding that informational text is best supported with realistic pictures that can provide more information. *Good readers learn new things from the illustrations and the words. Let's look at this illustration.* Turn to page 9. *The words tell us that zoos are made to be like the animals' natural homes. Look carefully at the illustration. What can you learn about a polar bear's home at the zoo?* Pause for responses. *Yes, we learned that polar bears live near water. Where did we find the evidence, in the words or the illustration? Awesome job, you know that good readers can learn new information from the illustrations. Let's write our new fact about polar bears in the L column of our KWL Chart.*

Continue to follow this routine of questioning, vocabulary building, and finding the evidence in the text and illustrations. Update the KWL Chart as you engage students in discussion during your group reading activities. When you finish the first read of this text, review your class KWL Chart. *Kindergartners, I am so very proud of you for being such superstar readers. Give yourself a cowboy! Yeehaw! We learned so many new things from this book because we kept asking and answering questions as we went along. Since it can be difficult to remember new facts, we used this awesome KWL Chart to help us organize our thoughts about this book. Let's see if we can remember some of those interesting new words and facts. When I say go, I want you to turn to a friend and share three things you learned from* Fun at the Zoo. Engage students in a turn and talk. Be sure to listen in and provide feedback to keep students on task. Afterward have several students share their ideas. Be sure to compare their new learning to the KWL Chart. *That is a great fact you learned. It is important we add the new information we learned to our L column. Class did we already write about zookeepers on our chart or should we add that to the L column?* Add new learning as needed.

Boys and girls, I think the author would be so proud of us. Do you know why? Yes, because the author wrote this book to teach us about zoos, and look at all of the cool things we learned. Point to the KWL Chart. *I think if we read this book again, we could learn even more new information about zoos. I usually read books two or three times so that I can learn lots. This time when I read it, I want to play the Grab It Game. Remember, to play this game, you will need to reach out and grab the new information. Catch it in your hand so you don't forget it!* Model stretching out your hand and grabbing the air. This kinesthetic strategy will actively engage students as you read and provide a prompt for remembering new information.

First, let's see if you remember the important parts of this book. I am going to give you a test! Have students identify the parts of the book as you point to the front cover, back cover, title, and title page. *Amazing job! Good readers know the parts of the book, and I can tell you are experts! Now we are ready to read and grab those new facts. Remember to listen for something different. That means listen for something new that we have not yet learned. Ready, switch on your searchlights and let's be information detectives!*

Read the entire book a second time. Pause and guide students to grab new information as you read. You may need to give some nonverbal signals like making your eyes really wide to cue students in when you are reading new facts. *I really like the way you are grabbing the new information and not even saying a sound. Keep holding it tight and let's see if we can discover anything else.* Continue this routine as you finish the second read of the book. Praise students for being awesome detectives. *Give yourselves some fireworks for being such awesome detectives for new facts. Good readers don't just sit and listen. They are always thinking about the words and the illustrations and trying to learn. I saw you grabbing some new information and I know that you are holding it tight right now. When I say go, turn to a friend and share what you grabbed. Turn to the front with your hands in your lap when you are done sharing. Go!* Have students turn and talk with a friend.

Provide corrective feedback and scaffolding as needed. Have students share responses with the whole group. Be sure to add new learning to the KWL Chart. Also remember to challenge students to explain the evidence behind their new learning. How do they know? Can they show you evidence from the words or the illustrations?

You are fantastic informational readers! You can ask and answer questions to help you learn new things. I love the way you helped me use the KWL Chart to organize our thoughts. First, we wrote down what we already knew about zoos. We put it right here in the K column. Then, we created lots of questions about things we wanted to learn in the W column. Last, in the L column, we wrote about what we learned.

I am so proud of you and I know the author, Molly Dise, would be so proud of you too for learning so much from her book. Do you know who else would be proud of you? Yes! Your family will think you are so smart. They love to hear about what you are learning at school. Let's make a KWL Chart about Fun at the Zoo *for you to take home and share with them. We wrote a lot of information in each column when we made this one as a class. When you make one to take home, you just need to pick one thing to write about in each column.* Model how to write in one idea for K, W, and L.

It is okay to have students copy your ideas. Remember, you want them to feel success. Some students will complete the KWL Chart independently with original kindergarten spelling while others will need much encouragement and support. All students will benefit from participating in the whole group comprehension lesson. The writing should be an extension and not a barrier. Accept all answers, and praise all writing response attempts! Positive reinforcement builds confidence and is a great motivator. Don't avoid this strategy because it is challenging. The more opportunities you provide for students to use this graphic organizer, the easier it will become for them to use it independently.

Center/Small Group Practice

Use these activities to engage students in practicing RI.K.1 and RI.K.2.

- **Writing Center:** Put out a variety of writing utensils and paper. Add nonfiction books. Encourage students to be superstar writers and write story pages or even books about the designated topic.

- **Role-Play Center:** Put out dress-up clothes and objects that students can use to role-play workers at a zoo, such as a zoologist or a veterinarian. Encourage them to present information about their jobs to the class.

- **Mural Center:** Put out a variety of writing materials and paper. Be sure to include one large poster-sized sheet of paper per group. Have students work collaboratively to draw a map of a zoo. Encourage them to label their mural too. Have zoo books available for a visual reference.

- **Guided Reading:** Put students in ability-level reading groups. Provide each member of your targeted group with the same appropriate leveled text. Review the KWL strategy. Now apply it in small group. Give each student a KWL Chart, and scaffold instruction as needed.

This kindergartner is role-playing being a veterinarian.

Independent Practice

Use these activities to engage students in practicing RI.K.1 and RI.K.2.

- **KWL Practice:** Have students complete a KWL Chart with any nonfiction read-aloud.

- **Nonfiction Writing:** Give students writing prompt pages that engage them in answering questions about your designated topic. Allow for differentiation by asking some students to add one word and others to write full sentences. You may need to provide different types of writing prompt sheets to allow for this differentiation. Sight word practice can also be embedded.

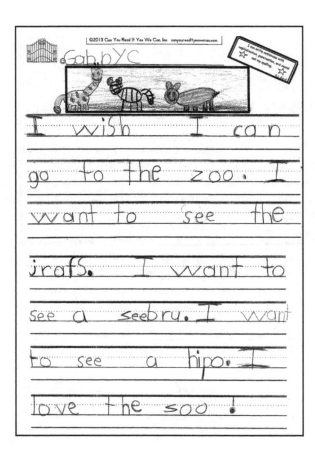

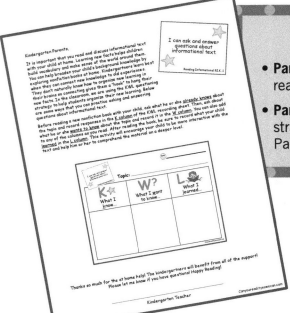

Figure 5.8 KWL Parent Newsletter
Full page available in Appendix

Parent Connections

- **Parent Night:** Model for parents how to get the most out of read-alouds at home. Show them how to use the KWL Chart.

- **Parent Letter:** After you have practiced the KWL comprehension strategy in the classroom multiple times, send home a KWL Parent Newsletter. (See Figure 5.8.)

Technology Tips

Use these activities to engage students in practicing RI.K.1 and RI.K.2.

- **View the Zoo:** Watch live streaming of a famous zoo online after having a text on the zoo read to them. Have children write about or draw what they see and add details from the book. Online sites can offer special experiences like a Panda Cam or teacher resources.

- **Computer Center:** Have students pick their favorite animal and become an animal expert. After researching the animal, have students make a slide show of animal facts. Set up a template with 4 or 5 slides so students include only the most important facts.

Children's Books to Teach Asking and Answering Questions

You can use the same routines in Lesson 2 to teach zoos using these books. Challenge students to make connections between fiction titles and nonfiction titles as well as make connections between nonfiction titles to support RI.K.9.

Fiction Titles

There's a Zoo in Room 22 by Judy Sierra, published by HMH Books for Young Readers

The View at the Zoo by Kathleen Long Bostrom, published by Ideals Children's Books

Nonfiction Titles

Zoo Animals by Brian Wildsmith, published by Star Bright Books

Zoo Animals by Patricia Whitehouse, published by Capstone

Zookeeper by Heather Miller, published by Capstone

Zoologists in the Field by Louise Spilsbury, published by Capstone

Reading Informational Assessment Checklist

- The ELA Assessment Checklist Reading Standards: Informational Text can be used while students are at play or engaged at literacy centers. (See Figures 5.5 and 5.6 on page 59.)

- This tool allows for open-ended use. Sometimes you might be observing the whole class for one indicated skill. Other times you might be analyzing one child on multiple skills. You can use a check mark or a date when skill is achieved.

- Use anecdotal records and notes while students are working independently or engaged in the classroom. You can place these notes in portfolios or digital portfolios.

CHAPTER 6

CAN YOU READ IT? YES WE CAN! Strategies for Teaching Reading Foundational Skills (RF.K)

Kindergartners have proven themselves to be more capable learners than we could ever have imagined. Years ago, early childhood educators focused classroom activities on sharing milk and cookies, getting along with others, listening to stories, and nap time. Children in preschool and kindergarten were often expected to merely play, print their names, paint, and practice social skills. Now we somehow need to weave in all of those developmentally appropriate experiences with high academic expectations. There is no debating that kindergartners need a strong literacy foundation in order to be successful learners. Young children need to understand how print works and be able to see the 1:1 correspondence between the spoken and written word. They also need to know the letters, sounds, and sight words. NAEYC (2009) underscores the importance of foundational skills in early literacy instruction in their Position Statement. "Compelling evidence has shown that young children's alphabet knowledge and phonological awareness are significant predictors of their later proficiency in reading and writing."

Kindergartners are challenged to develop so many new skills daily. To help them make isolated information concrete, we must teach the basic skills in tandem with authentic reading and writing. The creators of the Common Core Standards caution us to be careful not to view the foundational skills as an end, but rather as necessary components of a comprehensive literacy program. Instruction of foundational skills should occur in concert with reading, writing, speaking, and listening. The benefits of teaching these building blocks in context can reach far beyond the knowledge of isolated skills. Students who explore the features of print, letters, sounds, and sight words within real reading and writing gain confidence, enthusiasm, and higher-level comprehension. When foundational skill instruction is combined with authentic literacy experiences, learning is no longer limited and disconnected.

This kindergartner is a detective for punctuation marks as she reads the poem "Chester" in the pocket chart.

Purposeful application allows for differentiation too. Students who come to school already knowing skills like letters and sounds have the opportunity to be challenged by using those skills in reading and writing. Skill-infused reading and writing permits students to grow as individuals. Unfortunately, most reading curricula lack opportunities for kindergartners to apply foundational skills in independent reading and writing experiences. Curricula often include whole group verbal skill-and-drill practice but offer limited opportunities for children to be engaged in real reading and writing. Our challenge is to provide students with daily experiences that allow them to use the foundational skills as a vehicle to arrive at higher-level learning.

Think back to how you learned to ride a bike. Certainly you did not practice the important skills in isolation without ever getting on a bike. Pretending to pedal for hours one day and imaginary steering the next would never prepare you for the coordinated effort it takes to ride a bike. Hopefully someone helped you jump up on that bike and encouraged you to try all of the skills at once. Sure, that person probably first introduced you to the parts of the bike and maybe even provided you some training wheels. Most likely he or she walked right beside you, offering corrective feedback and reassurance at every tumble, twist, and turn. But this teacher never let you throw in the towel and always gave you lots and lots of opportunities to practice. Eventually, you could ride a bike without even thinking about all of the individual skills you needed to do simultaneously to be successful.

Learning to read and write is a lot like learning to ride a bike. We undoubtedly need to introduce students to foundational skills but we don't want them to sit stationary with their new information. They need to apply foundational skills in hands-on reading and writing experiences. Also, we need to deliberately provide corrective feedback and encouragement during actual literacy attempts in order to build each child's confidence and fluency. Independent learners who can make meaning from print in the world around them will emerge from repeated powerful practice. Foundational skills are essential and need to be taught systematically; but they must be taught within the context of real reading and real writing. Encourage your students to be brave like you were when you learned to ride a bike. Inspire your kindergartners to pick up that book and begin their first attempts at reading. Provide them feedback and positive reinforcement along their demanding yet joyful journey and watch them soar!

Print-Rich Environment

Kindergartners need to be surrounded with print that carries meaning. It is crucial to create a classroom environment that displays print abundantly. A print-rich environment contains schedules, labels, a reading corner, writing centers, word walls, and a variety of text reflecting multiple levels and topics. Children should be surrounded by big books, class made books, child made books, maps, recipes, letter tiles, writing boards, trade books, leveled readers, picture cards, anchor charts, poems, wordless books, alphabet books, songs, pocket charts, and so on. Encourage curiosity and ignite each student's natural sense of wonder about the world of literacy by inviting him or her to interact with print. Create walls that teach and inspire literacy learning everywhere.

Powerful Practice and Purposeful Play

The most powerful practice you can provide for young learners involves creating activities in which students can learn foundational skills as they make use of realistic reading and writing. This philosophy is highlighted by Bardige and Segal (2005), "For most, though, learning to read well is a process that takes many years and includes both explicit instruction and lots of playful, self-motivated practice with words, sounds, symbols, stories and books."

Children need to play with print. Embedding print within centers encourages students to use reading and writing in developmentally appropriate ways. Children come to school comfortable engaging in play. Take advantage of this prior knowledge to promote literacy learning in a setting where they naturally thrive. Ask your future chefs to read and write their own menus in the housekeeping center. Have upcoming architects label a mural or a map of your school. Stock your writing center with a variety of paper, pencils, crayons, staplers, and so on to inspire potential authors. Add paper to your block center for future engineers to draw and write about their designs. Put out photographs of student activities and encourage young journalists to narrate each class event in writing. Choose fantastically fun games that align to the Common Core's foundational skills that all students are eager to play every day.

Fill your classroom with friendship and family in an effort to create a familiar environment where kindergartners instantly feel safe to take risks and make mistakes. Nurture their social nature by encouraging literacy learning through interacting with one another. Children learn best when they have daily opportunities to use language. Applying the foundational skills as they communicate with one another allows students to enrich their understanding. Engage students in partner reading, collaborating to solve problems, and working together at literacy centers. Capitalize on every teachable moment to celebrate not only literacy success but also displays of kindness, compassion, and friendship. Collaborative play is a key component in helping students respect and support each other as they climb the ladder to literacy.

Reading and Writing Routines

Young children enter school eager to learn. Capitalize on their natural curiosity by immersing them in meaningful literacy experiences. Learning to read is a very complex process that needs to be strategically instructed. Kindergartners require simple structures and scaffold materials to help them be successful. Intentionally engage kindergartners in reading and writing routines repeatedly. Routines assure young children and help them build confidence when embracing new learning situations. Following familiar routines helps kindergartners be able to focus on new information without having to understand a new procedure too. Any skill or content area can be taught by using the following three reading and writing routines.

Routine 1: Teacher Shared Book Instruction

The first step is to design a patterned, predictable teacher book to use in a shared reading lesson. It is easy to create a book based on your targeted skill. Make a colorful, full-size laminated copy for whole group instruction. Teacher Shared books should be designed with limited text that focuses on key foundational skills, such as letters, sounds, rhyming, sight words, and word building. Integrate a gradual release of responsibility model. Kindergartners need much modeling and layered support before they are willing to take their own risks. The beginning pages of your book should include simple tracing of a targeted letter or word, while the last few pages should require students to write letters and words independently. (See Figure 6.1.)

Figure 6.1
I Am **Teacher Shared Book**
Available in color at
www.canyoureadityeswecan.com

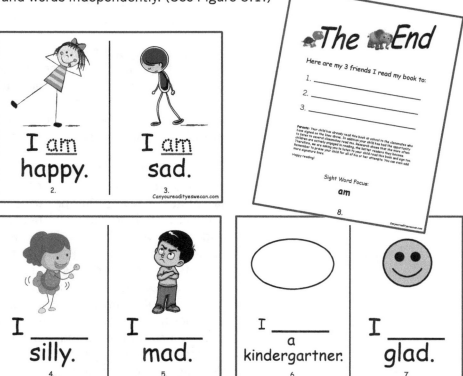

Always use this teacher tool first when implementing your routine during shared reading. Begin by drawing attention to as many foundational skills as possible. For example, point out the front cover, back cover, title, author, and so on. Before you read, encourage comprehension growth by using the Teacher Shared book to engage students in predicting, inferring, questioning, and connecting. Next, model fluent reading as you point to and read each word. Use a dry-erase marker to demonstrate tracing and writing the targeted letter/sight word. Also encourage students to echo read each page. Be sure to praise student attempts at reading to build confidence. Give students an opportunity to show they are superstar readers by inviting them to read the entire text with you as a group. To pump them up ask, "Can you read it?" and encourage them to respond with, "Yes we can!" This strategy sets the stage for students to be successful in reading the same book independently in Routine 2. After you have used a Teacher Shared book, it is crucial to place it in a reading corner or book bin. Kindergartners will enjoy reading it over and over again. Encouraging repeated reading will build student fluency and confidence. During independent reading time, students used to say, "But I can't read." Now every student feels like a reader and rushes over to grab one of the most recent Teacher Shared books and will read it with enthusiasm and pride!

Routine 2: Student Independent Practice/ Partner and Parent Read

In Routine 2, engage students in purposeful practice by having them complete an independent copy of the Teacher Shared book used in Routine 1. Simply make a black-and-white student sized copy of the Teacher Shared book for each child. Kindergartners will be very excited when you tell them that they get to make their very own copy to read to two friends and take home. Model expectations with a student copy.

Clip a student copy to your easel as you reread with the class. Remind students to print their names on the front cover and trace and write the targeted letter/sight word. Bring attention to the back cover. Explain that they are such amazing readers that they will now be able to read this book to two friends in the classroom. Friends should sign their names on the back of the student's book when they are done listening.

Engaging students in reading to friends in the classroom creates a community of readers. This purposeful practice is so powerful. Reading to classmates elevates this paper/pencil activity from being a typical skill-and-drill based worksheet to becoming an authentic literacy experience. Students develop their reading, writing, speaking, listening, and social skills simultaneously. It is so fun to walk through the classroom and hear students reading to friends with personality and passion. Additionally, this is a great opportunity for assessment. You can informally make observations or intentionally request that a student reads to you as you document his or her progress. It is amazing what you can learn about a student when you listen to him or her actively read an independent practice book. You can assess tracking print, fluency, fine motor skills, letter/sound knowledge, sight-word knowledge, memory, comprehension, and print concepts. These books are great for use in guided reading lessons too.

Now that students are filled with an enthusiasm for reading, they are encouraged to read their independent practice book with their families at home. On the back of their independent practice book, put a note explaining to parents that you have read this book in school and would like them to listen to their child read it at home. This parent involvement sparks school-related conversations between parents and children. A window of daily insight into the wonderful world of kindergarten opens for families. Parents used to ask what their child did during kindergarten because he or she always came home and stated, "I did nothing" or "I played with my friends." Now when parents read the independent practice book with their kindergartner, they know exactly what learning took place at school and what important skills to reinforce at home. Rarely can parents find at their local library just-right books that their children can read. They are limited to reading to their children rather than having their children read to them. Parents are so pleased when those just-right books magically come home every day.

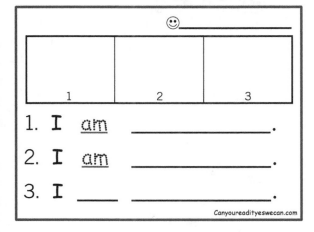

Figure 6.2
Writing Response
www.canyoureadityeswecan.com

Routine 3: Writing Response

In Routine 3, students make the connection to writing. After students have been exposed to the targeted letter/sight word through repeated readings with the Teacher Shared book and the independent practice book, they are ready to be authors. Create a writing response sheet that encourages practice of the targeted letter/sight word. (See Figure 6.2.)

When children write, they use higher-level thinking to apply foundational skills. Writing allows for differentiation and is the ultimate assessment tool. Student writing reveals application of letter/sound relationships, sight words, decoding, letter formation, print concepts, directionality, and so on. Kindergartners become empowered with excitement as they express themselves on paper.

Implementing this three step routine—Routine 1: Teacher Shared Book Instruction, Routine 2: Student Independent Practice/Partner and Parent Read, and Routine 3: Writing Response—creates a classroom community of engaged and independent learners. Students look forward to participating in shared reading and cheer with enthusiasm when they get to make their own books. They plead to read their books to more than two friends, and their parents are so proud when their kindergartners read at home. An additional benefit is that the writing routine ignites creativity and promotes risk-taking. When you routinely engage kindergartners in 180 days of authentic reading and writing, every student is excited to be a reader and eager to be an author. Using this reading and writing routine puts everyone at ease. Students and parents know exactly what to expect, which in turn sets everyone up for success in the learning community. When students are asked, "Can you read it?" they confidently respond, "Yes we can!"

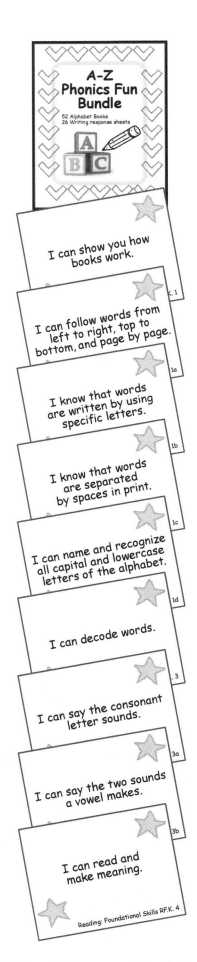

You should intentionally plan for incorporating multiple standards into a lesson. In Lesson 1, a phonics lesson can be used to bundle standards RF.K.1, RF.K.1a, RF.K.1b, RF.K.1c, RF.K.1d, RF.K.3, RF.K.3a, RF.K.3b, and RF.K.4. Also, since reading, foundational skills, writing, speaking, and listening are mutually reinforcing skills, several of these standard strand areas are naturally integrated in the lesson.

Lesson 1: Phonics

The Yy Songbook:
A-Z Phonics Fun Bundle

Published by www.canyoureadityeswecan.com

For this lesson, we are focusing on the letter Yy. You could apply the reading and writing routine to any letter of the alphabet.

Set the stage for standards learning. Begin the lesson by referring to the Let's Learn! wall and saying, *Kindergartners, look at the skills we are going to practice today.* Instill focus and enthusiasm for reading by having your students recite the day's posted learning targets. Continue with, *Why do you think we need to learn these skills?* Encourage students to respond with, "Because that is what good readers need to do." Cement the commitment of the class to reading by excitedly asking, *Who's a good reader?* Pump them up to respond "I'm a good reader!" Last, confirm their pledge by saying, *Yes, you are amazing readers. I am so proud of you. Now, let's learn.*

Gather kindergartners in the shared area. Remind students that great readers know how books work and they also know how to use letters and sounds to help them read and write. Establish that today you are going to practice the letter and sound for Yy. Some of your students will have prior knowledge about your targeted letter, whereas others will be learning about Yy for the first time. Therefore, it is crucial that you provide opportunities for the entire class to explicitly practice Yy in both isolation and in real reading.

Letters are so important because they help us read and write. Today we are going to practice reading and writing the letter Yy. Hold up a Yy alphabet card and have students echo name the letter as you point to it. Great job, this is capital Y and this is lowercase y. Now let's use our skywriting fingers to make a capital Y. Watch me first. Model for children how to write a Y as you talk them through the steps. *Now you are ready to try writing a capital Y. Get your skywriting fingers ready and let's make a capital Y together.* Talk students through making a capital Y. Repeat two times. Then, follow the same process for lowercase y. *Wow! I am so proud of you. You are superstar Yy writers! Give yourselves some fireworks! Whoosh!*

We are ready to practice the sound for y. When you see a y at the beginning of a word you should make the /y/ sound. Echo me, /y/. Provide corrective feedback if needed. *Let's sing some songs that help us practice the /y/ sound.* Sing any or all of the songs on the next page. These songs can be used for any letter of the alphabet. Just substitute the letter/sound you are targeting. Be sure to add fun kinesthetic movements like shoulder shaking or rainbow sparkle fingers.

My Name Is Y Rap Song

My name is Yy. My sound is /y/.
/y/-/y/-/y/ (shake shoulders)
/y/-/y/ (shake shoulders)

The Letter Yy

The letter Yy makes this kind of sound
/y/-/y/-/y/-/y/-/y/ (sparkle fingers in a rainbow arch)

Awesome job singers! What sound do we say when we see a letter Yy? Provide corrective feedback and re-teaching if necessary. *Now that we know the y sound, let's think of some words that begin with y. I'll go first. Yo-yo begins with y. Say it slowly with me, and let's stretch out the /y/ sound.* Sound out yo-yo slowly as you stretch your hand from your mouth. *Wow, I hear 2 y's. Did you?* Encourage students to generate more words that begin with the targeted sound. You can use a turn and talk and have students share with the class afterward. You can also print responses by recording their /y/ words on chart paper. *Now, I am going to test you and see if you are a /y/ expert. Listen carefully because I am going to try to trick you. We are going to play the thumbs-up, thumbs-down game. If I say a word that begins with /y/, give me a thumbs-up. If my word does not begin with /y/, give me a thumbs-down.* Provide students with practice words. This is a great way to informally assess students.

Now let's practice the letter and sound for y using this fun song in our pocket chart. (See Figure 6.3.)

Have students read the title as you point to it. *We are going make a song about the things we like best that begin with /y/.* Have children choral read the y word bank cards at the bottom of the chart. *Raise your hand if you would like to come up and put your favorite /y/ word in our song.* Take three volunteers. Then, have the class choral read/sing the entire song as you point.

Next, use the song to have students explore foundational skills within a real reading situation. *Kindergartners, let's be detectives for our important letter of the day, Y. Who can come up and point to a letter y in our pocket chart song?* Repeat for other print concepts like punctuation marks, words, or the title.

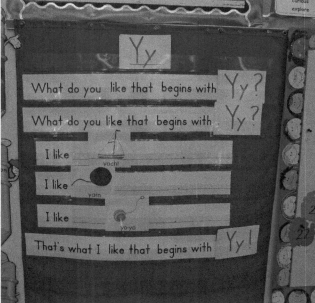

Figure 6.3 Yy Song

Implement Routine 1: Teacher Shared book. *I am so proud of you for being such amazing readers of this song. Give yourselves a cowboy. Yeehaw! We are ready to make a class book of the Yy song. Look, I made a book called The Yy Songbook.* (See Figure 6.4.) *Before we read it together, I am going to give you a test. What part of the book is this?* (front cover) Repeat for back cover and title.

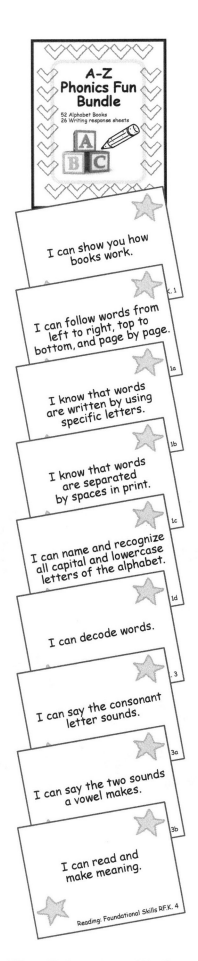

Figure 6.4 Front and Back Cover of Teacher Shared Book *The Yy Songbook*
A–Z Phonics Fun Bundle available in color at www.canyoureadityeswecan.com

Amazing job, kindergartners! Good readers know the parts of the book! You are good readers! If the title of this book is The Yy Songbook, *what do you think the book will be about?* Engage students in a turn and talk. Have them share predictions with a partner and then have several groups share with the class. *I like how you predicted that this book would have things that begin with the /y/ sound. The title gave us that clue. Awesome job readers!*

If I want to be a good reader, what do I do next? Facilitate a discussion about how to turn the pages properly and how to read from top to bottom and left to right. Try modeling the wrong way to follow print and have a student come up and show you the correct way. Kindergartners love to catch their teachers making a "mistake" and feel much pride when they model the right way to do something!

Okay, now that we know the parts of the book and which direction to go, I think we are ready to read. I will read first and then you can echo read. Read/sing pages 2 and 3 following the echo reading routine. (See Figure 6.5.)

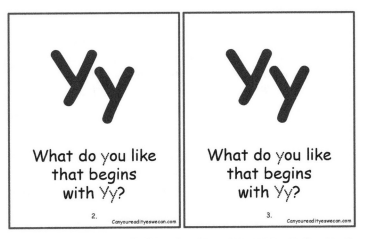

Figure 6.5 Pages 2 and 3 of Teacher Shared Book *The Yy Songbook*
Phonics Fun Bundle available in color at www.canyoureadityeswecan.com

Nice Job! This book is just like our pocket chart! I was wondering if you could be detectives for me? Who can come up and point to a letter for us? Great, Miguel. I like how you found the letter Y. Let's trace over the y's on these two pages. Get your skywriting fingers out, and I will use my special marker. Use a dry-erase marker and trace the Y's as you remind students how to print them. *You are experts at finding letter y's. Now let's practice finding a word. Remember words are separated by spaces and are usually made up of several letters. Look at this word. It is the word "do." It has two letters, d and o. Together d and o make the word "do." Can someone find another word on this page?* Have several students come up and point to words. *I love how you know how to be detectives for words. Give your-selves a round of applause.* Pause for students to clap. *Let's put those words together and read the sentence on each page.* Point and have students choral read.

Fantastic job superstar readers! Before I turn the page, make a prediction in your brain about what you think might be on the next page. Don't let your thoughts out. Keep them in your brain. Pause for silent predicting. Turn to pages 4 and 5 in *The Yy Songbook.* (See Figure 6.6.) Have students echo read pages 4 and 5.

Figure 6.6 Pages 4 and 5 of Teacher Shared Book *The Yy Songbook*
A–Z Phonics Fun Bundle available in color at www.canyoureadityeswecan.com

Did anyone predict that these pages would be about yogurt and a yo-yo? Nice job! Yogurt and yo-yo begin with what sound? Pause for the response of /y/. *What letter makes the /y/ sound? Yes, the letter y makes the /y/ sound. It is the special letter of the day. Who can be a detective for the y in yogurt and come up and trace it for us?* Invite a volunteer to share your dry-erase marker and trace the y on page 4. Repeat for page 5. *Let's give our helpers some fireworks. Whoosh! Very nice writing! Now let's read these two pages just like a kindergarten reading family. I'll be the pointer and you are the readers. Ready? Read.* Point and engage students in reading pages 4 and 5.

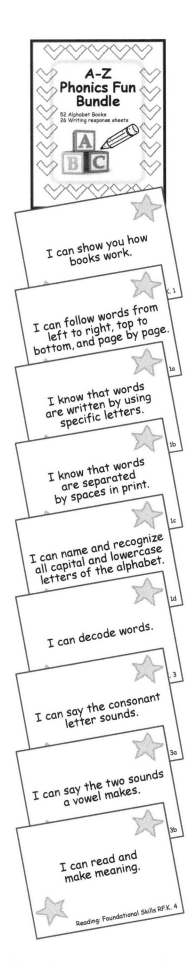

Awesome reading! Now, we are ready to read pages 6 and 7. Make a silent prediction about what you think they will be about. Then we will turn the page and check our predictions. Pause for time to predict. Then, turn to pages 6 and 7 in *The Yy Songbook.* (See Figure 6.7.) Discuss predictions.

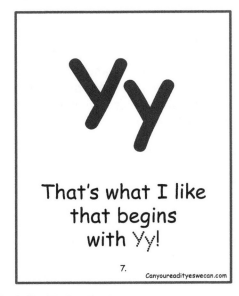

Figure 6.7 Pages 6 and 7 of Teacher Shared Book *The Yy Songbook*
A–Z Phonics Fun Bundle www.canyoureadityeswecan.com

Did you predict that there would be a blank page? Page 6 gives us a chance to be authors. We get to finish the sentence. What should we write about? Encourage students to think of things that begin with the letter y. *Yes we should write about something that begins with /y/ because that is what our book is all about. Turn to a friend and share an idea of something we should write on this blank line.* Engage students in a turn and talk. Discuss responses and pick one word to write together.

You had many great ideas. Let's choose one to write. Let's write "yams." We know that good writers stretch out their words and write down the letters for the sounds they hear. Let's use our fingers to catch the sounds we hear when we stretch out the word yams. Stretch out the word slowly as you put up a finger for each sound. Catching a sound with each finger gives students a kinesthetic way to remember the sounds. *Now let's write a letter for each sound. /y/—what letter do we need? Yes, we need a y first to spell yam so I will write a y first on the line. The word yams begins with y.* Repeat this process for the a-m-s. Provide scaffold support.

Nice job writers. Look we wrote the word "yams." What do you think we need to do here in this box? Point to the box on page 6. *Yes, we need to draw an illustration. Should I draw a dog? No! I need to make my illustration match my word. Since I wrote the word "yams," I have to draw an illustration of yams. Who can come up and draw yams?* Depending on students' vocabulary, you may need to describe it for them. Then, have a volunteer draw two yams in the box. Praise the illustrator. *What a superstar illustrator you are! Great job!*

We are ready to read page 7. I will read it first and you can echo read. Nice reading kindergartners. You are amazing. Did you notice anything at the end of this sentence? This sentence ends with an exclamation mark. Good readers use excited voices when they read sentences with exclamation marks. Let's try it again with our exciting voices. Choral read page 7 with enthusiasm! *Very nice!*

Turn to the back cover. (See Figure 6.8.) *What part of the book is this? Yes, it is the back cover. What does this say? The End. What an amazing job you have done reading our* Yy Songbook. *I like the way we were authors and wrote in the word "yams" too. Let's be superstar readers and read the whole book together without stopping this time. I will be the pointer and you be the readers. Can you read it?* Encourage students to respond, "Yes we can!" *Ready? Read.* Engage students in a fluent choral reading.

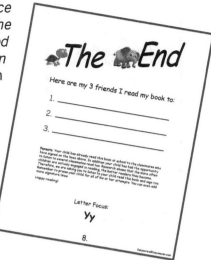

Figure 6.8 Back Cover of Teacher Shared Book *The Yy Songbook* **A–Z Phonics Fun Bundle www.canyoureadityeswecan.com**

Wow! You are superstar readers. Amazing readers don't just read the words, they also make meaning from the book. Amazing readers can tell someone what the book is all about. Was this book about swimming? No! This book was about something else. If you were trying to tell your family about this book, what would you say? Who can share an idea with the class? Encourage responses that summarize that the book is all about things that begin with /y/. Place the Teacher Shared book in your reading corner or book bin to facilitate repeated reading.

Implement Routine 2: Student Independent Practice/Partner and Parent Read.
I have some exciting news for you. You get to make your very own copy of The Yy Songbook. Display the Student Independent copy of *The Yy Songbook*. The student copy is a black-and-white reproducible of the Teacher Shared book used in Routine 1.

First, since you are going to be the author of this book, you need to write your name here by the smiley face. Model writing your name on the front cover. *What is the title of this book? You're right! It is called* The Yy Songbook. *It is exactly like my teacher book that we just read. Let's read it together and practice so you will be experts at making your own book. Remember, each time you see a letter Yy, you need to trace it. On page 6 you need to think of a word that begins with Yy and write it on the line. Don't forget to draw a matching illustration.*

Model tracing the y's and filling in the original response on page 6. Choral read *The Yy Songbook* with the class.

Fantastic job kindergartners! You are superstar readers and writers. Let's celebrate by sharing our great reading with each other. Kindergartners in a reading family like to read to their friends. When you listen to a friend read you should tell your friend that he or she is an awesome reader. In our reading family we show friends that they are great readers by signing our names on the back of their books after we listen to them read. Let's practice. Ask for a volunteer to be your friend, and model read your book. Have the volunteer tell you that you are a great reader. Then have the student sign his or her name on line one on the back of your book. (See Figure 6.9.) *Repeat for line two.*

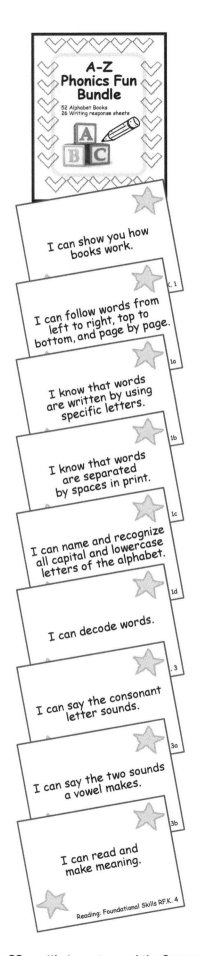

I can show you how books work.

I can follow words from left to right, top to bottom, and page by page.

I know that words are written by using specific letters.

I know that words are separated by spaces in print.

I can name and recognize all capital and lowercase letters of the alphabet.

I can decode words.

I can say the consonant letter sounds.

I can say the two sounds a vowel makes.

I can read and make meaning.

Miguel, thanks for being my reading friend. It makes my heart so happy that you listened to me read and signed your name. Notice that Miguel signed his name on the back cover of my book. Friends only sign on the back cover. Your name, the author's name, is the only name on the front cover of this book. Boys and girls did you notice that there is one more line on the back cover with a number 3. This is a very special line because this is where someone from your family will get to sign his or her name. There is a note right here, telling your parents that we read this book today at school and they should listen to you read it at home. Point to the parent note on the back cover.

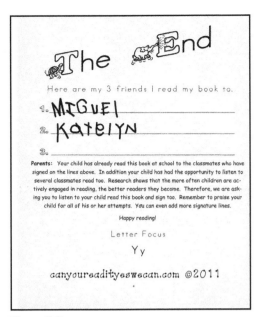

Figure 6.9
Back Cover of Student Independent Book
***The Yy Songbook* A–Z Phonics Fun Bundle**
www.canyoureadityeswecan.com

You are ready to make your own Yy Songbook. *Be sure to write your name on the front cover, trace the y's, write and illustrate something that begins with Yy, and color the pages. When you are finished making your book, be sure to read it to two friends.* Circulate as students are working and provide support and encouragement. You can use this as an opportunity for assessment. Observe a student reading to a partner or intentionally ask a student to read to you. Document your observations.

Implement Routine 3: Writing Response. If time allows, the writing routine can be completed on the same day or can be equally effective when completed on the next school day. Now that children are filled with ideas about things that begin with /y/, they will be more confident to write their own stories. *Kindergartners, you were amazing readers with your Yy songbooks! You are now ready to be amazing writers about the letter Yy.* Display a blank copy of the Yy Writing Response sheet on your easel. (See Figure 6.10.)

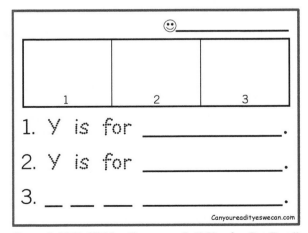

Figure 6.10 Yy Writing Response A–Z Phonics Fun Bundle
www.canyoureadityeswecan.com

Today you get to write three sentences about the letter Yy. First, write your name by the smiley face. Model how to do this for students. *Can you help me read sentence number one.* Point to the words as you encourage students to read the first sentence. Model tracing "Y is for."

Look, something is missing on this line. What could it be? Ask for volunteers. Model sounding out a word that begins with /y/. Encourage students to use their developmental spelling and accept student spellings. *Nice job! Let's read the sentence we wrote.* Read and point to sentence one. *Now you need to illustrate your Yy word in box number one. Make sure your illustration and your word match. Look, sentence two is just like sentence one. We need to trace the beginning words and then sound out one word that begins with /y/ at the end.* Model writing and illustrating sentence two. *Amazing writing! Let's read it.* Read and point to sentence two. *Kindergartners do you see anything different about sentence three? You are right. There are no clues to trace. You get to write the sentence all by yourself. What was the first thing that we wrote in sentences one and two? Yes! It was the letter Y. We need to write a Y first for sentence three.* Model writing the letter Y. Follow this routine for writing the words "is" and "for." *On the last line think of something else that begins with /y/. My favorite Y word is yogurt.* Model developmental spelling of yogurt and illustrate yogurt in box three. Engage the class in choral reading of sentence three.

Kindergartners, you are such amazing writers. I am so proud of you. Let's do the writing three to make sure your brain is ready to write your own Y story. Watch me first. I know that I need to think of three things that begin with the letter Yy to be able to write my story today. I am going to hold up a finger for each thing. Hold up a finger as you say each word: *yam, yo-yo, yogurt. Now it is your turn to do the writing 3. When I say "go," think of the three Yy things that you are going to write about today. Don't forget to hold up a finger for each one. Ready, go!*

Listen and provide scaffold support. *Wow! I heard some great ideas. I like how all of the ideas were different but all began with /y/. You are definitely ready to write and illustrate Yy words.* Send students to their tables to complete the Yy Writing Response sheet. Be sure to walk around and provide feedback and support. This is a great opportunity to assess writing skills and phonetic knowledge. Celebrate all writing attempts by allowing students to share in the Author's Chair or with a partner.

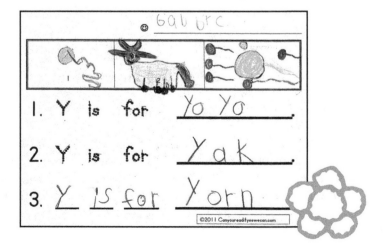

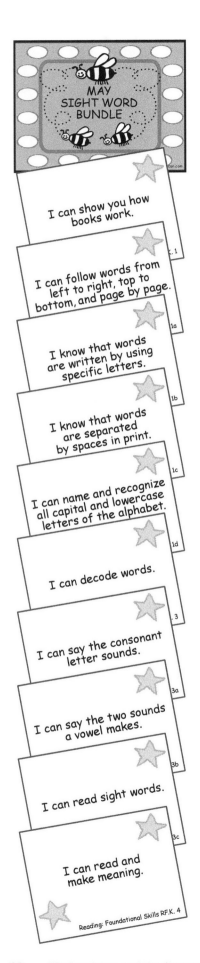

I can show you how books work.

I can follow words from left to right, top to bottom, and page by page.

K. 1

I know that words are written by using specific letters.

1a

I know that words are separated by spaces in print.

1b

I can name and recognize all capital and lowercase letters of the alphabet.

1c

I can decode words.

1d

I can say the consonant letter sounds.

3

I can say the two sounds a vowel makes.

3a

I can read sight words.

3b

I can read and make meaning.

3c

Reading: Foundational Skills RF.K. 4

You should intentionally plan for incorporating multiple standards into a lesson. In Lesson 2, a sight-word lesson can be used to bundle standards RF.K.1, RF.K.1a, RF.K.1b, RF.K.1c, RF.K.1d, RF.K.3, RF.K.3a, RF.K.3b, RF.K.3c, and RF.K.4. Also, since reading, foundational skills, writing, speaking, and listening are mutually reinforcing skills, several of these strand areas are naturally integrated in the lesson.

Lesson 2: Sight Words

Where Is The Bug?
The May Sight Word Bundle
Published by www.canyoureadityeswecan.com

This lesson focuses on the sight word "where." You can apply the reading and writing routine to any sight word.

Set the stage for standards learning. Begin the lesson by referring to the Let's Learn! wall and saying, *Kindergartners, look at the skills we are going to practice today.* Instill focus and enthusiasm for reading by having your students recite the day's posted learning targets. Continue with, *Why do you think we need to learn these skills?* Encourage students to respond with, "Because that is what good readers need to do." Cement the commitment of the class to reading by asking excitedly, *Who's a good reader?* Pump them up to respond "I'm a good reader!" Last, confirm their pledge by saying, *Yes, you are amazing readers. I am so proud of you. Now, let's learn.*

Kindergartners I have a super cool new word for you today. It is the word "where." Let's spell and clap it together. Point to a sight word card that contains the word "where." Clap and spell "where" as a class. Put "where" on the word wall. *Wow! You are great readers. Let's read "where" on the word wall now.* Using a pointer, engage students in reading "where" on the word wall. *"Where" is such an awesome word. I have a song that will help us remember how to spell "where." Echo sing with me.* Facilitate students in singing the "Where Song."

W-H-E-R-E (tune BINGO)
There is a word that we all know and where is its name-o.
W-H-E-R-E
W-H-E-R-E
W-H-E-R-E
School is where we like to go!

I love that song! Let's use our new song to play a game called "Mixed-Up Letters." Write the word "where" on a sentence strip. Sing the "where" song while pointing to the sentence strip. Next, cut apart the word into individual letters. *Kindergartners, the word "where" has five letters. We can cut them apart to play the Mixed-Up Letter Game. Boys and girls close your eyes. No peeking.* Mix up the letters in the word "where."

Open your eyes! Look what happened to the word. "Where" is all mixed-up. Can anyone come up and fix my word? Call a student up to the front to put "where" back together. Sing the "Where Song" as he or she fixes the word. *Friends, let's help Chloe and sing the "Where Song" as she puts our word back together for us. Great job Chloe! You are a superstar reader.*

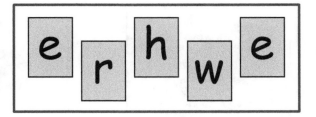

Implement Routine 1: Teacher Shared book. *I am so proud of you for being such amazing readers of this new word. Give yourselves a cowboy. Yeehaw! We are ready to make a class book using the word "where." Look, I have a book that has our new word of the day on it. Can you spy with your little eye the word "where" in the title? When you find "where" wiggle your fingers. Can anyone read the title? Let's read it together. Where Is The Bug?* (See Figure 6.11.) *Before we read the book together, I am going to give you a test. What part of the book is this?* (front cover) Repeat for back cover and title.

Amazing job, kindergartners! Good readers know the parts of the book! You are good readers! If the title of this book is Where Is The Bug? what do you think the book will be about? Engage students in a turn and talk. Have them share predictions with a partner and then have several groups share with the class. *I like how you predicted that this book would have bugs in it. Good readers always get clues from the title of a book.*

Let's look for a punctuation mark in the title. What is this called? Point to the question mark. *This is called a question mark. Use your skywriting finger and make one in the air with me. Question marks are used at the end of sentences when we ask a question. Our word of the day "where" is a special word that we can use to help us ask questions. For example, where is the bathroom? Or where is my pencil? Can you think of a "where" question sentence?* Share a few responses. *When we read* Where Is The Bug?, *let's be detectives for question marks.*

If I want to be a good reader, what do I do next? Facilitate a discussion about how to turn the pages properly and how to read from top to bottom and left to right. Try modeling the wrong way to follow print, and have a student come up and show you the correct way. Kindergartners love to catch their teachers making a "mistake" and feel much pride when they model the right way to do something!

Now that we know the parts of the book and which direction to go, I think we are ready to read. I will read first and then you can echo read. Read pages 2 and 3 following the echo reading routine. (See Figure 6.12.)

Figure 6.11 Front cover of Teacher Shared Book *Where Is The Bug?* May Sight Word Bundle available in color at www.canyoureadityeswecan.com

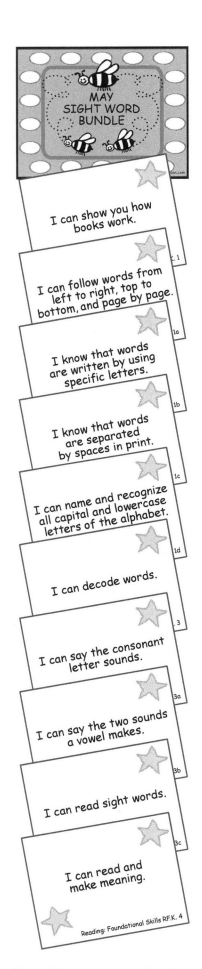

I can show you how books work.

I can follow words from left to right, top to bottom, and page by page.

I know that words are written by using specific letters.

I know that words are separated by spaces in print.

I can name and recognize all capital and lowercase letters of the alphabet.

I can decode words.

I can say the consonant letter sounds.

I can say the two sounds a vowel makes.

I can read sight words.

I can read and make meaning.

Reading: Foundational Skills RF.K. 4

Where is the ladybug?

2.

Where is the butterfly?

3.
Canyoureadityeswecan.com

Figure 6.12 Pages 2 and 3 of Teacher Shared Book *Where Is The Bug?* May Sight Word Bundle available in color at www. canyoureadityeswecan.com

Nice reading! I was wondering if you could be detectives for me? Who can come up and find the word "where"? Great job, Jamal. I like how you found our special word of the day. Let's trace over the word "where" on these two pages. Get your skywriting fingers out, and I will use my special marker. Use a dry-erase marker and trace the word "where." Then, sing the "Where Song."

You are experts at reading and writing the word "where." Are there other words on page 2? Let's figure out how many words are in this sentence? Remember that words are separated by spaces. Let's count together. Count how many words there are on page 2. *Friends, help me read the whole sentence now.* Repeat for page 3.

Fantastic job, superstar readers! Before I turn the page, make a prediction about what you think might be on the next page. Don't let your thoughts out. Keep them in your brain so everyone has a chance to think. Pause for silent predicting. Turn to pages 4 and 5 of *Where Is The Bug?* (See Figure 6.13.) Have students echo read pages 4 and 5.

_____ is the ant?

4.

_____ is the beetle?

5.
Canyoureadityeswecan.com

Figure 6.13 Pages 4 and 5 of Teacher Shared Book *Where Is the Bug?* May Sight Word Bundle available in color at www. canyoureadityeswecan.com

Did anyone predict that these pages would be about an ant and a beetle? Nice job! Did you notice that something is missing on these pages? Raise your hand and wiggle your fingers if you know what word should go on the lines. Yes! It is the word "Where." Class, can you sing to me about how to spell the word "Where"? Invite a volunteer to share your dry-erase marker and write in the word "Where" on page 4. Remind students to use a capital W because "Where" is the first word of the sentence. Repeat for page 5. *Let's give our helpers some fireworks. Whoosh! Very nice writing! Now let's read these two pages just like a kindergarten reading family. I'll be the pointer and you get to be the readers. Ready? Read.* Point and engage students in reading pages 4 and 5.

Awesome reading! Now, we are ready to read pages 6 and 7. Make a silent prediction about what you think these pages will be about. Then, we will turn the page and check our predictions. Pause for time to predict. Then, turn to pages 6 and 7. (See Figure 6.14.) Discuss predictions.

Did you predict that there would be a bee? I like the way the author put all the bugs on page 7. I didn't predict that. But look, our special word is missing again. What word should we write on the lines? Yes, the word "Where" is missing. Class, can you sing to me about how to spell the word "Where"? Invite a volunteer to share your dry-erase marker and write in the word "Where" on page 6. Remind students to use a capital W because "Where" is the first word of the sentence. Repeat for page 7. Note that "where" on page 7 needs to have a lowercase w. *Let's give our helpers some fireworks. Whoosh! Very nice writing! Now let's read these two pages just like a kindergarten reading family. I'll be the pointer and you get to be the readers. Ready? Read.* Point and engage students in reading pages 6 and 7.

_____ is the bee?

Here we are _____ everyone can see!

6.   7.
Canyoureadityeswecan.com

Figure 6.14 Pages 6 and 7 of Teacher Shared Book *Where Is The Bug?* May Sight Word Bundle available in color at www.canyoureadityeswecan.com

Turn to the back cover. (See Figure 6.15.) *What part of the book is this? Yes, it is the back cover. What does this say? The End. What an amazing job you have done reading Where Is the Bug? Let's be superstar readers and read the whole book together without stopping this time. I will be the pointer and you be the readers. Can you read it?* Encourage students to respond, "Yes we can!" *Ready? Read.* Engage students in a fluent choral reading.

Wow! You are superstar readers. Amazing readers don't just read the words, they also make meaning from the book. Amazing readers can tell someone what the book is all about. Was this book about school? No! This book was about something else. If you were trying to tell your family about this book, what would you say? Who can share an idea with the class? Encourage responses that summarize that the book is all about bugs and helps us learn the word "where." Place the Teacher Shared book in your reading corner or book bin to facilitate repeated reading.

The End

Here are my 3 friends I read my book to:

1. _____
2. _____
3. _____

Parents: Your child has already read this book at school to the classmates who have signed on the lines above. In addition your child has had the opportunity to listen to several classmates read too. Research shows that the more often children are actively engaged in reading, the better readers they become. Therefore, we are asking you to listen to your child read this book and sign too. Remember to praise your child for all of his or her attempts. You can even add more signature lines.
Happy reading!

Sight Word Focus:
Where

8.
Canyoureadityeswecan.com

Figure 6.15 Back Cover of Teacher Shared Book *Where Is The Bug?* May Sight Word Bundle www.canyoureadityeswecan.com

Implement Routine 2: Student Independent Practice/Partner and Parent Read. *I have some exciting news for you. You get to make your very own copy of* Where Is The Bug? Display the Student Independent book of Where Is The Bug? The student copy is a black-and-white reproducible of the Teacher Shared book used in Routine 1.

First, since you are going to be the author of this book, you need to write your name here by the smiley face. Model writing your name on the front cover. *What is the title of this book? You're right! It is* Where Is The Bug? *It is like my teacher book that we just read. Let's read it together and practice so you will be experts when you make your own book. Remember our special word in this book is "where." Sometimes you will need to trace "where" and sometimes you will get to write it all by yourself.* Model tracing and writing in the word "where." Then, choral read *Where Is The Bug?* as a class.

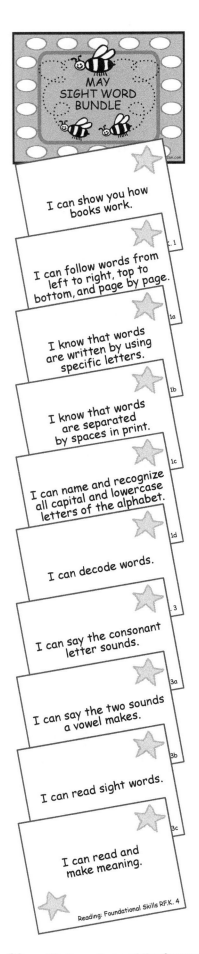

I can show you how books work.

I can follow words from left to right, top to bottom, and page by page.

I know that words are written by using specific letters.

I know that words are separated by spaces in print.

I can name and recognize all capital and lowercase letters of the alphabet.

I can decode words.

I can say the consonant letter sounds.

I can say the two sounds a vowel makes.

I can read sight words.

I can read and make meaning.

Reading: Foundational Skills RF.K. 4

Fantastic job kindergartners! You are superstar readers and writers. Let's celebrate by sharing our great reading with each other. Kindergartners in a reading family like to read to their friends. When you listen to a friend read, you should tell your friend that he or she is an awesome reader. In our reading family we show friends that they are great readers by signing our names on the back of their books after we listen to them read. Let's practice. Ask for a volunteer to be your friend, and model read your book. Have the volunteer tell you that you are a great reader. Then have him or her sign on line one on the back of your book. (See Figure 6.16.) Repeat for line two.

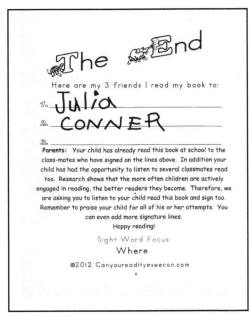

Figure 6.16 Back Cover of Student Independent Book *Where Is The Bug?* May Sight Word Bundle www.canyoureadityeswecan.com

Remember, friends only sign on the back cover of your book. Your name, the author's name, is the only name on the front cover of the book. Boys and girls, did you notice that there is one more line on the back cover with a number 3. This is a very special line because this is where someone from your family will get to sign his or her name. There is a note right here, telling your parents that we read this book today at school and they should listen to you read it at home. Point to the parent note on the back cover.

You are ready to make your own Where Is The Bug? *book. Be sure to write your name on the front cover, trace and write the word "where," and color the pages. When you are finished making your book, be sure to read it to two friends.* Circulate as students are working and provide support and encouragement. You can use this as an opportunity for assessment. Observe a student reading to a partner or intentionally ask a student to read to you. Document your observations.

Implement Routine 3: Writing Response. If time allows, the writing routine can be completed on the same day or can be equally effective when completed on the next school day. Now that children are familiar with how to read and write the word "where," they will be more confident to write their own "where" stories.

Kindergartners, you were such amazing readers with the book Where Is The Bug? *I really enjoyed listening to you read. You are now ready to be amazing writers.* Display a blank copy of the "where" Writing Response sheet on your easel. (See Figure 6.17.)

Today you get to write three "where" sentences about bugs. Let's pretend we are going on a bug hunt. First, don't forget to write your name by the smiley face.

Can you help me read sentence number one? Point to the words as you encourage students to read the first sentence. Model tracing *"Where is the."* Look, something is missing on this line. What could it be? It is the name of the bug we are hunting for first! What bug should it be? Ask for volunteers. Model sounding out a word that completes the sentence.

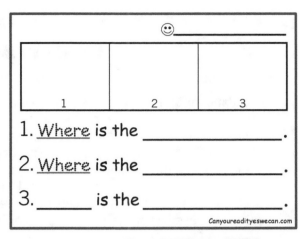

Figure 6.17 "Where" Writing Response May Sight Word Bundle www.canyoureadityeswecan.com

Encourage students to use their developmental spelling and be accepting of student spellings. *Nice job! Let's read the sentence we wrote.* Read and point to sentence one. *Now you need to illustrate your writing in box number one. Make sure your illustration and your word match. Look, sentence two is just like sentence one. We need to trace the beginning words and then sound out our bug word at the end.* Model writing and illustrating sentence two. *Amazing writing! Let's read it.* Read and point to sentence two. *Kindergartners do you see anything different about sentence three? You are right. There are two blank lines this time. What is the first thing that we wrote in sentences one and two? Yes! It was the word "Where." We also need to write in the bug word for the sentence. I really like butterflies. Let's sound out butterfly.* Model writing and illustrating sentence three. Model developmental spelling of *butterfly.* Then, engage class in choral reading of sentence three.

Kindergartners, you are such amazing writers. I am so proud of you. Let's do the writing three to make sure your brain is ready to write your own story. Watch me first. I know that I need to think of three bugs to be able to write my story today. I am going to hold up a finger for each bug. Hold up a finger as you say each word: *ant, bee, butterfly.*

Now it is your turn to do the writing 3. When I say "go" think of three bugs that you are going to write about today. Don't forget to hold up a finger for each one. Ready, go!

Listen and provide scaffold support. *Wow! I heard some great ideas. You are definitely ready to write about and illustrate some bugs. Let's review our important word of the day.* Sing the "Where Song." *The word "where" will be in each of our sentences too. You are ready to be superstar writers.* Send students to their tables to complete the "where" Writing Response sheet. Be sure to walk around and provide feedback and support. Praising a variety of responses will encourage creativity and risk-taking. This is a great opportunity to assess writing skills and phonetic knowledge. Celebrate all writing attempts by allowing students to share in the Author's Chair or with a partner. You can even display writing on a bulletin board or make a class book to spark ownership and enthusiasm!

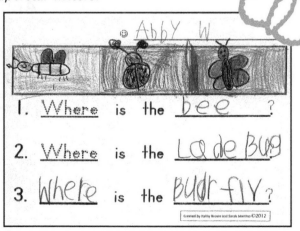

Center/Small Group Practice

Use these activities to engage students in practicing RF.K.1d, RF.K.2a–e, and RF.K.3a–d.

Foundational Skill Centers: Use the games listed below to create centers with enough pieces for 6 players. It helps if you color code the game boards so that students can easily keep the materials organized. Your students will love the activities and you will love how easy it is to implement the Common Core Standards with fun and developmentally appropriate centers! Games for the following standards are shown below: I can count, pronounce, and segment syllables in words (Figure 6.18); I can decode words (Figure 6.19); and I can read common high-frequency words by sight (Figure 6.20). Games such as these can be played during whole group as part of a phonemic or phonological awareness lesson, in small group, or independently after it is instructed.

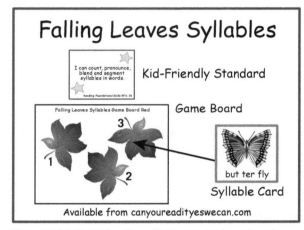

Figure 6.18 Example of a syllable center idea found in Apples and Leaves Common Core Kit at www.canyoureadityeswecan.com

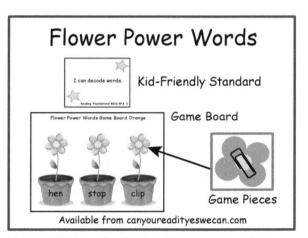

Figure 6.19 Example of a decoding center found in Flowers and Frogs Common Core Kit at www.canyoureadityeswecan.com

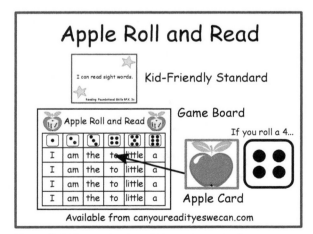

Figure 6.20 Example of a sight word center found in Apples and Leaves Common Core Kit at www.canyoureadityeswecan.com

Independent Practice

Use these activities available from www.canyoureadityeswecan. com to engage students in practicing RF.K.1d, RF.K.2a–e, RF.K.3a–d, and RF.K.4.

- **Sight Word Books and Writing Response Sheets:** Create books and writing response sheets that engage students in using a targeted sight word. Embed sight-word practice within a meaning print experience to help students practice reading, writing, speaking, and listening simultaneously! It is easy to bundle multiple Common Core Standards and inspire reading and writing enthusiasm. First, have students trace the keyword followed by repeated reading opportunities. This scaffold results in students reading and writing the targeted word independently. Then, build reading excitement by having students read to classmates and family members. Last, allow students to be authors and use the targeted sight word in their own writing piece.

- **Alphabet/Phonics Books and Writing Response Sheets:** Have students create alphabet books to help them recognize the letters Aa–Zz and produce the letter sounds. Books that focus on phonics will help develop vocabulary and engage students in emergent text that is authentic and fun. First, have students simply trace the targeted letter, and eventually have them write original stories about the letter. This is a great assessment of their phonics knowledge.

- **Life Science Content Books and Writing Response Sheets:** Use emergent readers to help students practice a targeted sight word and develop content knowledge. It is also a fantastic opportunity for authentic reading and writing. Since sight-word practice is embedded within a book format, students practice reading, writing, speaking, and listening simultaneously! Plus, life science content like growing things, habitats, and life cycles inspire students to want to read these books repeatedly. Activities like these align with multiple Common Core Standards and will inspire reading and writing enthusiasm.

Parent Connections

- **Parent Night:** Model for parents how to reinforce reading foundational skills like phonemic awareness, phonics, and sight words at home.

- **Parent Letter:** Create parent newsletters to send home as you teach important skills in the classroom. Parents are usually willing to practice but they do not always know what to do. Be specific and supply word lists to help them be successful. (See Figures 6.21 and 6.22.)

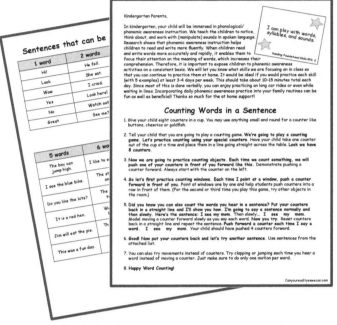

Figure 6.21 Words in a Sentence Parent Newsletter and Sentences, Full page available in Appendix

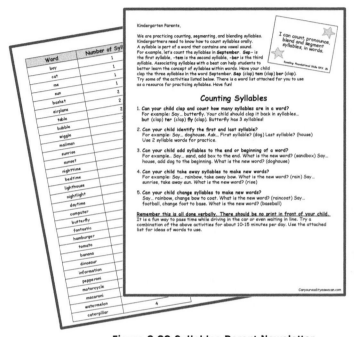

Figure 6.22 Syllables Parent Newsletter and Words, Full page available in Appendix

Technology Tips

Use these activities to engage students in practicing RF.K.1d, RF.K.2a–e, and RF.K.3a–d.

- **Apps Here, Apps There, Apps Everywhere:** There are many different apps that can be used in the classroom. Whether you project them on a big screen or use them as a center, apps are a great way to meet the needs of your struggling kindergartners as well as students who need to be challenged.

- **Websites:** Just like apps, there are many websites that can be used to provide fundamental skills practice in fun, engaging ways. Skills like letter/sound identification, syllables, rhyming, and blending and segmenting are often the focus of popular website games. Just do a search for kindergarten website games. Be sure to play the games first as a class before having students play independently.

- **Earobics Software:** Earobics is a great software tool that engages students in practicing phonological and phonemic awareness skills. Earobics automatically adjusts to each player's skill level and provides differentiated practice.

Children's Books for Teaching Foundational Skills

Great Books for Rhyming

Big Red Barn by Margaret Wise Brown, published by HarperFestival
Creepy Critters by Rebecca Rissman and Sian Smith, published by Capstone
Fox in Socks by Dr. Seuss, published by Random House
I Saw an Ant on the Railroad Track by Joshua Prince, published by Sterling
Moo, Baa, La La La! by Sandra Boynton, published by Little Simon
My Truck Is Stuck by Kevin Lewis, published by Hyperion Books for Children
Noisy Nora by Rosemary Wells, published by Viking
Rhyming Dust Bunnies by Jan Thomas, published by Beach Lane Books
The Going to Bed Book by Sandra Boynton, published by Little Simon

Great Books for Teaching the ABC's

Alphabet Under Construction by Denise Fleming, published by Square Fish
Chicka Chicka Boom Boom by Bill Martin Jr. and John Archambault, published by Little Simon
Dr. Seuss's ABC: An Amazing Alphabet Book by Dr. Seuss, published by Random House
Eating the Alphabet by Lois Ehlert, published by HMH for Young Readers
Everyday Alphabet series by Rebecca Rissman and Daniel Nunn, published by Capstone
Phonics Fun A–Z, published by canyoureadityeswecan.com
The Alphabet Tree by Leo Lionni, published by Dragonfly Books
The Letter Books, published by Capstone
Z Is for Moose by Kelly Bingham, published by Greenwillow Books

Great Books for Teaching Sight Words and Decoding

Animal Babies ABC: An Alphabet Book of Animal Offspring by Barbara Knox, published by Capstone
Big and Small Animals by Ann Corcorane, published by Capstone
Bob Book series by Bobby Lynn Maslen, published by Scholastic
Brave Fire Truck by Melinda Melton Crow, *published by Capstone*
Brown Bear, Brown Bear, What Do You See? by Bill Martino Jr, published by Henry Holt and Company
Go Dog. Go! by P.D. Eastman, published by Random House
Green Eggs and Ham by Dr. Seuss, published by Random House
Oh My Oh My Oh Dinosaurs! by Sandra Boynton, published by Workman Publishing Company
One Fish, Two Fish, Red Fish, Blue Fish by Dr. Seuss, published by Random House
Sight Word Bundles, published by canyoureadityeswecan.com
The Foot Book: Dr. Seuss's Wacky Book of Opposites by Dr. Seuss, published by Random House

Reading Foundational Skills Assessments

- Use the ELA Assessment Checklist Reading Standards: Foundational Skills while students are at play or engaged at literacy centers. (See Figure 6.23.)

- Use the Authentic Reading Assessments to record observations when students are engaged in real reading. (See Figure 6.24 for phonics books and Figure 6.25 for sight word books.)

- Use the Authentic Writing Assessment to record observations of writing. (See Figure 6.26.)

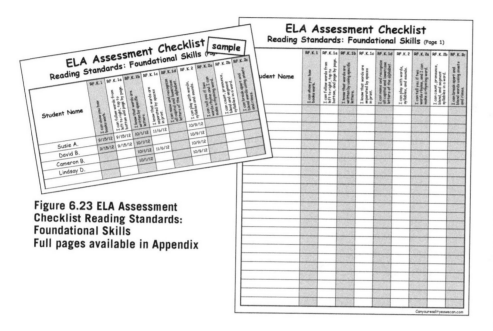

Figure 6.23 ELA Assessment Checklist Reading Standards: Foundational Skills
Full pages available in Appendix

Student: _____ Date: _____

Authentic Reading Assessment

Using any simple reader, mark the following criteria:

Skill	Satisfactory	Developing
Can the student identify the front cover of the book? Say, **Show me the front cover of the book.** (RI.K.5)	+	✓
Can the student identify the back cover of the book? Say, **Show me the back cover of the book.** (RI.K.5)	+	✓
Can the student identify the title of the book? Say, **Show me the title of the book.** (RI.K.5)	+	✓
Does the student know that print is read from left to right? Say, **Which way do I go? Where do I read next?** (RF.K.1a)	+	✓
Can the student identify a targeted letter in the book? Say, **Show me a letter___ Or What is this letter?** (RF.K.1d)	+	✓
Can the student identify a word in the book? Say, **Show me a word that you know and tell me what it is.** (RF.K.1c)	+	✓
Can the student identify an illustration in the book? Say, **Show me an illustration.** (RI.K.7)	+	✓
Does the student know the meaning of a period? Point to a period in the text. Say, **What is this and what do I use it for?** (L.K.2b)	+	✓
Does the student have one-to-one match with voice to print? Say, **Watch as I point and read the words.** Model pointing and reading the words for pages 2 and 3. Say, **Now it is your turn.** Point and read the rest of the book. (RI.K.10)	+	✓
Can the student make meaning of the text? Say, **Tell me, what was this book all about?** You might have to prompt with tell me more or what else did you learn? (RF.K.4)	+	✓

Notes:

Figures 6.24 and 6.25
Authentic Reading Assessments
Full pages available in Appendix

Student: _____ Date: _____

Authentic Writing Assessment

For use with any writing paper. Mark the following criteria:

Skill	Satisfactory	Developing
Did the student begin **writing** (an opinion or information) after the prompt or was extra support needed to generate ideas? (W.K.1-2)	+	✓
Did the student use a correct **pencil grip** and form letters correctly? (L.K.1a)	+	✓
Did the student use **directionality** when writing? (Start at the left and go to the right and start from the top to the bottom.)	+	✓
Did the student write **more** than one sentence about the topic?	+	✓
Did the student use a **capital letter** at the beginning of the sentences? (L.K.2a)	+	✓
Did the student use correct **spacing** within sentences?	+	✓
Did the student use appropriate **punctuation** at the end of sentences? (L.K.2b)	+	✓
Did the student use correct **spelling** when writing high **frequency words**?	+	✓
Did the student attempt to use **developmental spelling** on non-high frequency words? (L.K.2c-d)	+	✓
Did the student's **illustration** reflect the sentences written?	+	✓
Was the student able to read the sentences back and construct meaning from his or her work?	+	✓

Notes:

Figure 6.26
Authentic Writing Assessment
Full page available in Appendix

Student: _____ Date: _____

Authentic Reading Assessment: Sight Words

Using any of the books to mark the following criteria:

Skill	Satisfactory	Developing
Can the student identify the front cover of the book? Say, **Show me the front cover of the book.** (RI.K.5)	+	✓
Can the student identify the back cover of the book? Say, **Show me the back cover of the book.** (RI.K.5)	+	✓
Can the student identify the title of the book? Say, **Show me the title of the book.** (RI.K.5)	+	✓
Does the student know that print is read from left to right? Say, **Which way do I go? Where do I read next?** (RF.K.1a)	+	✓
Can the student identify a letter in the book? Say, **Show me a letter that you know and tell me what it is.** (RF.K.1d)	+	✓
Can the student identify a word in the book? Say, **Show me a word that you know and tell me what it is.** (RF.K.1c)	+	✓
Can the student tell what an illustration depicts? Say, **Describe what this illustration tells us about.** (RI.K.7)	+	✓
Does the student know the meaning of a period? Point to a period in the text. Say, **What is this called and what do I use it for?** (L.K.2b)	+	✓
Can the student identify the **targeted sight word** in the book? (Use a flash card or the book to point to the word and have student identify targeted sight word.) (RF.K.3c)	+	✓
Does the student have one-to-one match with voice to print? Say, **Watch as I point and read the words.** Model pointing and reading the words for pages 2 and 3. Say, **Now it is your turn.** Point and read the rest of the book. (RI.K.10)	+	✓
Can the student make meaning of the text? Say, **Tell me, what was this book all about?** You might have to prompt with tell me more or what else did you learn? (RF.K.4)	+	✓

Notes:

CHAPTER 7

WHO'S A SUPERSTAR WRITER? Strategies for Teaching Writing and Language (W.K and L.K)

Young children are fascinated by the thought of writing and have a deep desire to become members of the grown-up writing world! They instantly feel pride and empowerment when they craft their first markings of meaning. Kindergartners enter school with a wide range of literacy skills. Nevertheless, each and every student beams with accomplishment the first time he or she sits in the Author's Chair.

Writing is a complex process that not only conveys messages but also evokes emotion. For years, early educators feared that writing instruction would fail unless students first could recognize all letters and sounds and even some sight words. Now, we know we can't wait; we must kindle each kindergartner's burning desire to be a writer on the first day of school. Owocki and Goodman (2002) encourage teachers to help their students feel the power of writing. "Children who feel the power of writing and feel positive about themselves as writers are likely to want to write and to make an effort to communicate effectively in writing."

Don't wait for the perfect time to begin writing instruction. Dive in on day one. Engaging your students in expressing themselves through writing will add energy, empowerment, and excitement to your learning community. The power of the pencil is contagious. When your students catch the superstar writing bug, they will truly blossom with literacy learning.

Establish an Environment of Empowered Writers

As elementary educators, we have been carefully trained on the important pieces of the writing puzzle that must be addressed in our curriculum. The dilemma specifically facing kindergarten teachers is how do we implement instruction about specific writing strategies when our students do not really write yet? We can't help students improve their voice or sentence fluency if they are not able to put their thoughts on paper. Even our brightest students who enter school reading usually do not write sentences. Beginning of the year writing lessons typically call for students to write about themselves or their families. This all sounds simple until I hear the cries of, "but I don't know how to write," that echo around the room. Then I see the students' eyes begin to tear up. Every student seems to need me at the same time, and I begin to panic realizing there is not enough of me to go around. Unfortunately, my students quickly pick up on my frustration and now relate anxiety to the process of writing. Undoubtedly, kindergartners need something more before they can jump into writing. So, where do we start?

First, create an environment where students are encouraged to take the risk to write. Never underestimate the power of persuasion, and use it in every word you speak in the classroom! The magic is in choosing words that will motivate. Young children want to please their teachers and tend to become what we tell them they are. Why not tell them they are superstar writers? If you are all accepting and encouraging and believe that your students are writers, then they will believe it too. Don't worry about conventions with beginning kindergarten writing. You must first focus on helping students develop a writer's attitude. Experts like Owocki and Goodman (2002), who have researched emergent writing behavior, emphasize the importance of establishing empowered writers. "Children who come to see their writing as something that is not neat enough, not conventional enough, not connected to their lives, or not meaningful in the real world are likely to be unmotivated to write, and if their experiences are negative, they may avoid taking the risks that are requisite to their growth."

★ Superstar Writers! ★

Make sure your students feel positively about writing on day one of school. Have children sign a class poster as they enter the kindergarten doors. High five every student after he or she attempts to write on the class poster and say, "Wow, you are a superstar writer!" Something so simple can set an attitude to build upon for future writing success. Later in the day refer back to the poster. Hang up the poster and say, "I am so proud of all of you. What a nice job you did. Look, we are a kindergarten family of superstar writers! Superstar writers are kindergartners who try their very best when they write. I love the way you were all superstar writers on this poster. Way to go! Give yourselves some fireworks! You are all superstar writers!"

This creates a concrete experience of accomplishment related to writing. Students feel empowered instead of anxious about the process of writing. Each time you begin a writing lesson, be sure to take advantage of the superstar praise to pump up your students before they begin the difficult task of putting thoughts on paper. "Today, superstar writers, we are going to write about our families. Give yourselves a cowboy for being superstar writers! Remember, I am so proud of you when you try your very best. You are not an adult so you do not have to write like a grown-up. You are a kindergartner. Kindergartners use their kindergarten superstar writing. Being a kindergarten superstar writer means all you have to do is try your best. You can draw pictures. You can write letters, words, or sentences to tell about your family. When you are done, you can share your writing with the class. We will celebrate all of your amazing writing by cheering for everyone. Who's a superstar writer? Yes, you are all superstar writers. Now superstar writers, let's go write!"

This magical motivating talk is what is missing in early childhood writing curricula. Take the time to plant the seeds of empowerment and watch your writers grow!

After helping students take on a writer's attitude, it is now essential to find out where on the developmental writing continuum each child is functioning. Kindergarten teachers can't simply build on a previous curriculum or the previous teacher's recommendations because each of our students enters the classroom with a different experiential background. Instead, we must become familiar with the developmental stages that all children experience in an effort to set goals for individualized instruction.

Young children go through a series of stages when they begin to write. There are characteristics for each step along the way like scribbling, making shapes, drawing pictures, writing random letters, labeling, spelling phonetically, and so on. Many of these stages are predictable, but the lines between them can be blurry as each child paves his or her own unique path in reaching writing milestones. We must carefully analyze our students' writing and celebrate their successes while setting challenging but achievable goals for growth. Give students open-ended writing opportunities so that you can easily see the range in abilities. If you only ask students to copy a sentence that you have written on the board, you will only find out if they are capable of copying. To gather information on each student's full writing potential, engage your students in authentic writing, and collect their writing samples. For instance, after having students write about their families, have them share their work in the Author's Chair. Pay attention to what they write and carefully listen to how each student "reads" what was written. One student may simply draw a picture and make some random scribbles. Another student may draw a picture and write " I lvmi momdad." Both students state that their writing says, " I love my mom and dad." As a teacher I can gain so much writing insight from this activity. The first student obviously needs help learning letters and sounds to express her writing; whereas, the second student is ready for instruction about spacing and punctuation.

Use the developmental steps as a road map to help guide differentiated writing instruction for your students. Be sure to respect each child's developmental stage and honor his or her efforts. Your role should be that of a commanding coach as well as a continuous cheerleader.

Talk with Your Pencil

Children have messages to share long before they are capable of writing them on paper. Young children primarily talk to express their thoughts and needs. It is essential that we teach kindergartners that writing is a special kind of talking. Writing is simply talking with your pencil.

Model share this "talking" by writing. "I really want to tell you that I like kindergarten. I can use my voice and say it out loud, or I can talk with my pencil by writing that I like kindergarten. Watch me talk with my pencil." Write: I like kindergarten.

"Writing is just using your pencil to talk. I bet you have many things that you like too. Who wants to come up and share an idea? I will help us talk with our pencil and write it." Take several volunteers and model writing with your pencil.

Kindergartners need to see the connection between oral and written language to understand the purpose of writing. Writing becomes "lifework" when students see its function in communicating their thoughts and not just something that you do as schoolwork. Also help your students understand the difference between handwriting and writing. Handwriting solely involves the formation of letters. Writing involves expression and is powerful because it conveys a message. Have students help you label your classroom so that they can see how written words represent real objects in the world.

Make sure you have important print everywhere. A kindergarten classroom should have the following print pieces clearly accessible: the alphabet in multiple places, including on the wall and on portable strips; classmates' names and pictures; class lists; center labels; signs; sight words; posters; schedules; anchor charts; and children's work displayed. Fill the walls with print that your students can make connections to so that they feel ownership in their classroom. Refer to environmental print often so students begin to use it independently to support their attempts at talking with their pencils.

Engage your students in writing whole class dictation stories to help them build their written word awareness. Point out print concepts as you talk out loud to model writing. Also use their thoughts so that they are invested, but make sure you model the actual writing. For example, if you are studying colors, write a class story about red. Take dictation and model writing the kindergartners' sentences. Discuss directionality, spacing, sounding out, and so on. Talking out loud as you write will provide a concrete model of the writing process that kindergartners need. They will see the one-to-one correspondence between the spoken and written word. Follow a gradual release

Figure 7.1: This kindergartner writes, "Red is a bracelet. Red is a necklace. Red is an earring."

of responsibility model and have students eventually write their own red story. Encourage them to talk with their pencils and share their favorite red things. (See Figure 7.1.) Don't forget to display their red stories. Children will be motivated to read them repeatedly in class books or use reading pointers to track the stories displayed on the wall.

Morning messages are another great tool to help kindergartners see the connection between the spoken and written word. Prewriting a message and posting it on your easel will spark instant engagement from your class. They will want to know what message has been written to them. Use morning messages to ignite enthusiasm about the day's events and to model the writing process. Make it interactive by having students come up and circle targeted sight words or punctuation marks or having volunteers track the print with special pointers as the class reads the message aloud. Kindergartners lack prior reading and writing experiences. Providing authentic contexts like dictated stories or morning messages helps students think actively about print. The end result is the development of a deeper awareness of words, spelling, and the conventions of written language.

Evoke Emotion

Kindergartners require routines and meaningful opportunities to practice writing. Young learners need daily experiences to explore and experiment with writing for a variety of purposes and audiences.

Writing also needs to be an interactive process. Kindergartners must feel like they are part of a writing community that respects and supports one another. Make the most of this social nature to create writers who are regularly involved in collaborative conversations about writing. Kindergartners who respect each other's ideas and are open to learning from one another become well-rounded thinkers.

Writing becomes powerful the moment it is shared in the classroom. When another student encourages a classmate by stating, "I love your writing. That was a great idea," it evokes pride in the author. Kindergartners who are supported by one another are motivated to continue to write. The more opportunities you give your students to share their writing, the more opportunities they have for positive interaction. Engage kindergartners in writing for a variety of purposes, such as poetry, songs, stories, recipes, letters, research reports, and so on. Simply creating a greeting card center can allow students to express many meaningful emotions. Kindergartners can write "happy" cards to cheer up a classmate or "congratulations" cards for a friend who has a new baby brother. Try assigning a daily reporter to write about and share classroom events. Students will beam with excitement when it is their turn.

Capitalize on the kindergartners' creativity. Allow them to become playwrights and watch their stories entertain, capturing the attention of an entire class. Don't skip the sharing. Have your students read their writing to a variety of audiences, such as the principal, other teachers, reading buddies, community members, parents, and so on. When students receive feedback on their writing, they are inspired to be superstar writers.

I love Mrs Brow
She is Pite
and botFlay
So N iS

Your words are extremely powerful in inspiring a classroom of mutual respect and compassion for one another. It is important to routinely tell students how happy they make your heart when they write messages. When students know you care about them, they care about learning. Teachers hold motivation in the palms of their hands. All you have to do is open your fingers and release words of encouragement while your students are engaged in writing. Watch as the power of praise transforms each student into confident, creative, capable writers. IRA and NAEYC (1998) underscore the importance of the writing community in their Joint Position Statement: "In classrooms built around a wide variety of print activities, then in talking, reading, writing, playing and listening to one another, children will want to read and write and feel capable that they can do so."

The reciprocal respect fueled by a supportive writing community enables young learners to take the risk to write.

Read to Write/Write to Read

Reading and writing are mutually reinforcing skills that must be taught in tandem. Children innately love to listen to literature. Take advantage of your kindergartners' natural curiosity about books by carefully choosing read-alouds that you can use to coach your students into being accomplished writers.

Young children lack prior knowledge and experiences with writing. Kindergartners are often filled with fear about the idea of composing thoughts on paper. They require concrete examples that provide clear expectations of the writing process in order to inspire them to take the risk to write independently. Use books to teach your children about what an author does. Start with a book like *Rocket Writes a Story* by Tad Hills. Use this book to provide background information about how to write a story. Your students will instantly connect with the main character and be inspired to write.

Use books like *Alexander and the Terrible, Horrible, No Good, Very Bad Day* by Judith Viorst to stimulate conversations about character development. Follow up by engaging students in writing a response about their favorite character. Read texts like *Owl Moon* by Jane Yolen to talk about using descriptive words when writing about the setting of a story. Reading *I Wanna Iguana* by Karen Kaufman Orloff is an effective prompt to not only teach letter writing but also to model persuasive writing. Reading a nonfiction text like *Chicken and Egg* by Christine Back and Jens Olesen can spark kindergarten scientists to record facts and information. Intentionally take the time after every read-aloud to celebrate something specific about the author's craft and watch your writers ignite. Comment enthusiastically to motivate kindergartners to write. For example, "Wow, I love the way the author used color words to describe objects in this story. I really want to write a story using color words sometime." You will be amazed at how many of your students will choose to write a color story that very day during center time.

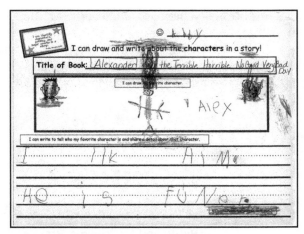

Student response about a favorite character

Writing reinforces reading. When children write they are actively engaged in using letters and sounds to make meaning. Encoding words helps children be stronger decoders when they read. The reciprocal relationship between reading and writing must be respected. Venn and Jahn (2003) remind us, "Teachers and researchers soon found that by experimenting with the writing process—by trying to encode with letters and symbols—children became more able to decode as well as write. Thus, the reciprocity of reading and writing behaviors in young readers was recognized as an essential component of early literacy instruction." Don't isolate reading and writing instruction. Your students will benefit from seeing the bigger picture when you use reading to help your children write and writing to help your children read.

Student responding to a read-aloud

You should intentionally plan for incorporating multiple standards into a lesson. In Lesson 1, a response to literature writing lesson can be used to bundle standards W.K.1, L.K.1, L.K.1a, L.K.1f, and L.K.2a–d. Since reading, foundational skills, writing, speaking, and listening are mutually reinforcing skills, several of these standard strand areas are naturally integrated in the lesson.

Lesson 1

Hey, Little Ant
by Phillip and Hannah Hoose
Published by Tricycle Press

For this lesson, we are focusing on a response to the book *Hey, Little Ant* by Phillip and Hannah Hoose. You could apply this reading and writing routine to any read-aloud.

Set the stage for standards learning. Begin the lesson by referring to the Let's Learn! wall and saying, *Kindergartners, look at the skills we are going to practice today.* Instill focus and enthusiasm for reading and writing by having your students recite the day's posted learning targets. Continue with, *Why do you think we need to learn these skills?* Encourage students to respond with, "Because that is what good readers and writers need to do." Cement the commitment of the class to learning by excitedly asking, *Who's a superstar learner?* Pump them up to respond, "I'm a superstar learner!" Last, confirm their pledge by saying, *Yes, you are superstars! I am so proud of you. Now, let's learn.*

Gather kindergartners in the shared area. Draw student attention to the class superstar sign-in poster from the first day of school. *Boys and girls do you remember our superstar writing poster? We are a family of superstar writers. Who remembers what a superstar writer does?* Accept all responses and encourage students to remember that superstar writers simply try their best. *I am so proud of you when you try your very best. You are not an adult so you do not have to write like a grown-up. You are a kindergartner. Kindergartners use their kindergarten superstar writing. Being a kindergarten superstar writer means all you have to do is try your best. Today we are going be superstar writers. Give yourselves a cowboy, superstar writers! Yeehaw!*

Engage students in a discussion that previews the purpose of the writing lesson. Students will need to write a response, sharing their opinions about what the kid should do at end of the story *Hey, Little Ant.* Display the front cover of the book. *I know two authors, Phillip and Hannah Hoose, who need our help. They wrote this fantastic book called* Hey, Little Ant, *but they don't know how to end their story. Can you help them? Let's read this story to see if we can help the authors. Be careful listeners as I read so that you will be able to share your ideas at the end.*

Discuss print concepts, such as title, author, illustrator, and so on. Engage students in making predictions using the front cover. Continue to monitor predictions throughout the story. Stop periodically to discuss the author's and illustrator's craft. Ask students how the illustrations support the text to bring greater meaning. Can they find the evidence? Can they make inferences? Discuss the meaning of new vocabulary like *squish, crook, nest mates,* and so on. Use turn and talks or whole class discussions to engage students in higher-level thinking. Encourage comprehension by intermittently asking questions such as, *Why did the illustrator make the kid so big and the ant so small? Why did the author use rhyming words so often? Can you make a connection to the kid or the ant, and why? Have you ever thought about how an ant has a family too? Do you know what bullying means? Is one of the characters in this story being a bully? Is the book fiction or nonfiction? How do you know?* Encourage students to follow up their responses by explaining and showing evidence from the text. It is the discussion that occurs during the reading of this text that will set students up for successful writing responses later. Talk is the springboard to writing.

Save the last page of the text to discuss explicitly. *Kindergartners, this is the last page of the book where the authors need our help. Listen carefully as I read.* Read the last page of *Hey, Little Ant.* The authors leave the kid with the raised up shoe and ask what the kid should do. This is a great opportunity to engage students in discussion. *Pretend you are the kid. Lift up your shoe. The ant is right below. What are you going to do? Turn to a friend and share your thoughts. Don't forget to tell your friend why you think your idea is the best choice. There is no right or wrong answer. It is an opinion. An opinion is a statement that tells how you feel about some-thing. It is OK that we have different opinions. Remember, we are giving our ideas about how to help the authors end the story. This isn't happening in real life. We are helping to write a pretend adventure.* Engage students in a turn and talk. Circulate and listen to responses. Praise a variety of responses that are well explained. Give plenty of time to talk, as talk is the rehearsal for writing.

Choose at least two different responses to share in whole group. *Wow! You have some fantastic opinions about how the story should end. I really liked hearing all of the different ideas you had. Your opinions are powerful when you explain why you made your choice. Nicky, I loved when you said the kid should stomp on the ant because an ant bit you one time and you are afraid of ants. You told us what the kid should do and why you think that. Telling why makes it a great opinion. Hannah, your opinion was different from Nicky's but awesome too. You said you would not smoosh the ant because you felt sorry for the ant. Nice job sharing your opinion, Hannah.*

Hannah and Nicky did an amazing job sharing their opinions. I know all of you have some awesome opinions too. Let's be superstar writers and share our opinions on paper. Remember writing is just talking with your pencil. You already shared your opinion by talking with a friend. Now it is time to talk with your pencil and write your thoughts on paper. Don't forget, super-star writers try their best. You can draw pictures. You can write letters, words, or sentences to tell your opinion.

Let's practice by writing an opinion together. We are going to use this special paper to write our opinion about Hey, Little Ant. *I need to write my name by the smiley face first.* Use any formatted paper that your students are familiar with. Add a note at the top to inform parents about your writing prompt.

Next, we need to think of a whole sentence to express our opinion. We can't just write one word like "kid" or "ant." One word doesn't give enough detail and doesn't tell you my opinion of what I think the kid should do. Listen to my whole sentence. The kid should squish the ant. Do you know what I think the kid should do? Yes, because I told you a complete sentence. Now we need to write the sentence on our paper. Let's clap and count the number of words we will need. Model clapping and counting the number of words in your first sample sentence. Have students clap and count the words in the sentence with you.

Great job! There are six words in my sentence. I need to talk with my pencil and write the first word on my paper. What was the first word in my sentence? You're right. My first word was "The." Is "The" a word wall word that I can copy. It is! Who can come up and point to "the" on the word wall. Can you spell "the" out loud as Nina points? You talk and I will write with the pencil. I am going to start writing the first word right here at the top of the paper. Write "The" on the paper. *I used a capital T because "The" is the first word of our sentence. Capital letters are the big letters. The small "baby" letters cannot lead a sentence. We always have to start our sentences with a BIG capital letter.* (See Figure 7.2.)

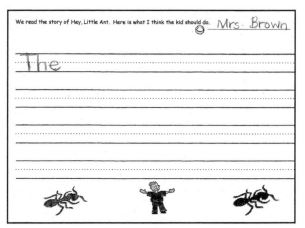

Figure 7.2 Teacher Model Writing for *Hey, Little Ant*

Nice job helping me write "The," the first word in our sentence. Give yourselves some fireworks for being superstar writers. What is the next word that we need to write? Let's clap the words in our sentence to help us remember. Clap and count the words in your first sample sentence: The kid should squish the ant. *Super job, friends! The next word we need to write is "kid." Is "kid" a word wall word? No, "kid" is not on our word wall. We will need to use our kindergarten spelling to sound out the word "kid." Remember, when we use our kindergarten spelling we stretch out a word by saying it slowly. We use our fingers to catch the sounds and then we write a letter for each sound. Let's say the word "kid" slowly, /k/-/i/-/d/. Hold up a finger as you say each sound. What sound did we catch first?*

Yes, it was /k/. What letter do we need to write to represent the /k/ sound? Students may respond with c or k. *You are right, both c and k can make the /k/ sound. The word "kid" actually begins with a k, so let's write k. Where can we look in our classroom if we need help writing a k?* Point to the alphabet display in your classroom. *Great job! You can use the alphabet strip on the wall or on your desk to help you write letters.*

Where do I write the word "kid"? Yes, I have to write "kid" after the word "The." But it is really important that I do not let the two words touch. I have to leave a space between my words or they will get all jumbled together. Model what would happen if your words touched and how meaning would be lost. *If my words touched they would get mixed together and my writing wouldn't make any sense. Watch me leave a two finger space in between the words "The" and "kid."* Place two fingers after the word "The." Then write a k after your two fingers. *Fantastic job, writers. Don't forget to leave two finger spaces between your words when you write today.*

Continue sounding out the remaining letters in "kid." Follow the same routine, modeling spacing and kindergarten spelling until you finish your sample sentence. Provide much praise and encouragement to inspire confidence in your future writers as you implement this shared writing activity. After writing the last word you will need to discuss punctuation. *This is great! We finished writing our sentence but I think something is missing at the end. Superstar writers always put punctuation marks at the end of their sentences. I am going to put a period at the end of this sentence to show that my sentence is finished. I like to call a period a "stop dot" because it is a dot that I can use to mark the end of my sentence. Draw a period in the air with your magic finger while I write one with my pencil.* Model writing a period at the end of your sentence. (See Figure 7.3.)

Note that we model phonetic spelling, so some of the words are not spelled correctly. Modeling phonetic spelling is critical in encouraging students to take the risk to write. Kindergartners feel empowered when they use their kindergarten spelling to convey messages. Conventional spelling emerges as reading and writing skills develop.

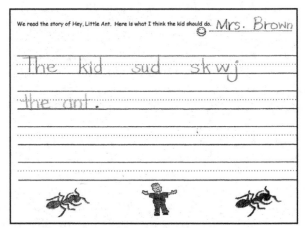

Figure 7.3 Teacher Model Writing for *Hey, Little Ant*

I can write about my opinion about a book or topic.

Writing W.K. 1

I am a superstar speaker and a superstar writer.

Language L.K. 1

I can write my capital and lowercase letters.

Language L.K. 1a

I can share my ideas in complete sentences.

Language L.K. 1f

I can write sentences using capital letters, punctuation, and kindergarten spelling.

Language L.K. 2a-d

Now that we have finished writing a whole sentence let's read it together. The kid should squish the ant. *Point to each word as you read. I love how you were all superstar writers. You helped me think of a whole sentence. Then we used a capital letter at the beginning of our sentence. We wrote word wall words. We even used our kindergarten spelling to sound out new words. We were careful to use two finger spaces and even added a period at the end of our sentence. We did everything a superstar writer would do. Let's give ourselves a round of applause.*

Now we can make our opinion more powerful if we share why we think the kid should squish the ant. I think he should squish the ant because the ant stole the family's picnic food and needs to be stopped! Let's write he was bad and took the food. Remember good writers don't just write one word. Superstar writers write complete sentences. Engage students in helping you write this new sentence. Follow the same routine as the sample sentence 1. (The kid should squish the ant.) Focus on the conventions targeted in the lesson standards. Be sure to read the entire opinion response with the class. Praise all efforts to encourage future writers. (See Figure 7.4)

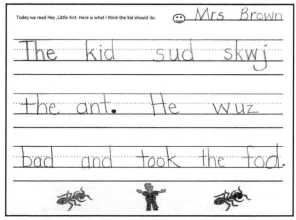

Figure 7.4 Teacher Model Writing for *Hey, Little Ant*

I am so excited because now it is your turn to talk with your pencils and share your opinions. To help your brain get ready for writing I want you to turn and talk with your friend about what you are going to write today. We have shared lots of different opinions. You are the author, so you get to choose how the story will end. Don't forget, a powerful opinion tells why you made your choice. When I say "go," turn to your friend and share your powerful opinion. Go. Listen to responses. Provide scaffold support to ensure that all students have formulated an idea and will be ready to write.

Awesome ideas! I am so excited to see how you will put your talk on paper. I can't wait to read all of your opinions. You can use your pencil to draw pictures and write letters, words, and sentences. Remember to be a superstar writer and try your very best. When you are done, you can share your writing with the class. We will celebrate all of your amazing opinions by cheering for each other. Who's a superstar writer? Yes, you are all superstar writers. Now superstar writers, let's go write!

Remove your paper from the easel so that students do not copy your work. They will naturally want to copy your paper if it remains in front of them. Remind students that you accept all responses as long as they try. Writing is not copying. The end goal is not to copy the class sample but to share an original opinion. Circulate and provide differentiated support. Some students will simply need some words of encouragement. Others will need more intensive support to sound out words. Be cautious not to spell words for your students. Instead teach them where to find words on the word wall and how to use their kindergarten spelling. Empower your students to be independent writers. Don't give up if this task is difficult the first few times. Your students will become more independent writers with ample opportunities and enthusiastic encouragement. Challenge higher-level writers who might finish early to include more conventions and details in their work.

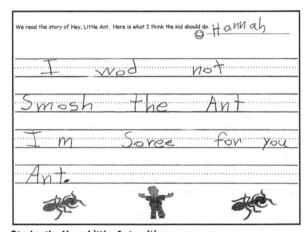

Student's *Hey, Little Ant* writing response

When students are finished, encourage them to share their opinion writing in the Author's Chair. Clip student writing to your easel so that students feel empowered as they assume the role of the teacher. Provide a superstar pointer for superstar writers to use when sharing their work. Your students will exude pride and excitement when they sit in the Author's Chair. Celebrate each child's attempts at being a writer. Lead listeners in providing positive praise about each friend's writing. When students hear their peers say, "I love your writing" or "Nice job, you remembered your two finger spaces," they are inspired to continue to grow as a writer.

Continue to foster a kindergarten community of writers. Intentionally create opportunities for students to share their writing with a wide variety of audiences, such as the principal, other teachers, reading buddies, parents, an online pen pal, and so on. Display student writing on bulletin boards and in class books so its message can be enjoyed repeatedly.

Sharing is the vehicle that transports student writing from a piece of paper into the world of active communication. Feedback stimulates dynamic classroom conversations filled with voice and passion. When kindergartners share their written work they not only learn about writing but also about each other. Ultimately, students in a collaborative classroom writing community will develop as readers, writers, and friends.

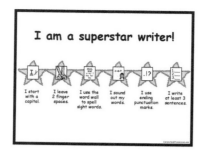

I am a superstar writer!

I start with a capital. | I leave 2 finger spaces. | I use the word wall to spell sight words. | I sound out my words. | I use ending punctuation marks. | I write at least 3 sentences.

Intentionally plan for incorporating multiple standards into every lesson. Lesson 2 is an editing lesson, and it can be used to bundle standards W.K.5, L.K.1, L.K.1a, L.K.1f, and L.K.2a–d. Since reading, foundational skills, writing, speaking, and listening are mutually reinforcing skills, several of these standard strand areas are naturally integrated in the lesson.

Lesson 2

Superstar Writing Rubric

Published by www.canyoureadityeswecan.com

For this lesson, we are focusing on editing a piece of narrative student writing. You could apply this routine to any type of writing previously written in the classroom.

Set the stage for standards learning. Begin the lesson by referring to the Learning Wall and saying, *Kindergartners, look at the skills we are going to practice today.* Instill focus and enthusiasm for writing by having your students recite the day's posted learning targets. Continue with, *Why do you think we need to learn these skills?* Encourage students to respond with, "Because that is what good writers need to do." Cement the commitment of the class to learning by excitedly asking, *Who's a superstar writer?* Pump them up to respond "I'm a superstar writer!" Last, confirm their pledge by saying, *Yes, you are superstars! I am so proud of you. Now, let's learn.*

Gather students in your shared area. *Boys and girls, it has been so exciting to hatch chicks in our classroom. Yesterday was especially awesome when we each got to hold a baby chick for the first time. It was really amazing to write about our experience. Your writing was very interesting and your messages were clear. Beginning writers sometimes choose a special story they have written to polish up and make even better. They reread their writing and look to see if they have done everything a superstar writer should do. Polishing up your writing is called editing. Editing your writing makes it sparkle! It reminds me of when you clean your toys. They become sparkly and new and everyone wants to play with them. Editing helps your writing look better and makes it easier to read. Editing your work makes everyone interested in reading it.*

I can edit my writing to make it better.

Writing W.K. 5

I am a superstar speaker and a superstar writer.

Language L.K. 1

I can write my capital and lowercase letters.

Language L.K. 1a

I can share my ideas in complete sentences.

Language L.K. 1f

I can write sentences using capital letters, punctuation, and kindergarten spelling.

Language L.K. 2a-d

Today we are going to edit our chick writing. Let's practice together by editing my story. Display your writing on the easel. *I know I did a good job but I can always make my writing better. Editing works best when you have a friend to help you. It is fun to have a polishing partner that gives ideas about how to sparkle up your writing. Will all of you pretend to be my polishing partners and help me make my chick writing sparkle? Thanks! I am so excited to edit my chick story.*

First we need to think about what good writers do. Draw student attention to the class superstar sign-in poster from the first day of school. *Do you remember our superstar writing sign-in poster? We are a family of superstar writers. Who remembers what a superstar writer does?* Accept all responses and encourage students to remember that superstar writers simply try their best. *I am so proud of you when you try your very best. You are not an adult so you do not have to write like a grown-up. You are a kindergartner. Kindergartners use their kindergarten superstar writing. Being a kindergarten superstar writer means all you have to do is try your best. I know that you tried your very best when you wrote your chick stories. Give yourselves a cowboy, superstar writers! Yeehaw!*

I made this Superstar Writer Chart to help us edit our writing. (Figure 7.5.) *It shows us what a superstar writer needs to do. It says right up here at the top, I am a superstar writer! Each star reminds us of an important thing a writer must do to make his or her message clear when writing. Let's look at the first star. The picture has a capital I and a lowercase i with a line through it. Writers, what do you think this could be reminding us to do? Yes, right here it says, "I start with a capital." We know that the baby lowercase letters can't lead a sentence. Class, let's make a promise to always start our writing with a capital letter. Kindergartners raise your hand and say it with me. "I start with a capital letter." Awesome! Let's look at the next star and see if we can figure out what else superstar writers should always do. I see two fingers in the picture. Who can tell us what this star might be reminding us to do?*

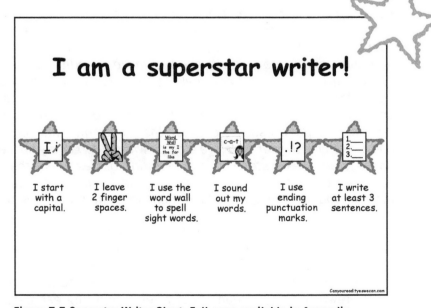

Figure 7.5 Superstar Writer Chart, Full page available in Appendix

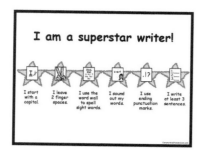

Continue the same process as you discuss each star on the Superstar Writer Chart. Be sure to use the pictures as prompts for discussion to instill ownership in the writing process. Have students echo read each sentence under every star too.

Fantastic job class! This chart tells us six things that we need to do when we write to be superstar writers. You read them as I point. Engage students in choral reading the entire chart. *Awesome! Wow! This chart helps us remember so many important things about being a good writer that I am going to hang it up right here on the wall so that we can always see it. I also made some smaller copies of the chart and hung them up by your tables so that you have them near you when you write. Six stars can be a lot to remember, so just find a chart to look at whenever you need help!*

Now that we know what superstar writers should do, let's check my writing and see if I was a superstar writer. Read your chick writing aloud as you point to each word. (See Figure 7.6.)

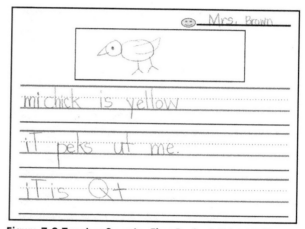

Figure 7.6 Teacher Sample: First Draft of Chick Writing

I think I did a good job but I know I can make it better. Since you are my polishing partners, I need you to help me shine it up. Class, what was the first thing a superstar writer does? Yes, it was using capital letters. Oh no, I forgot to start my sentences with capital letters. Can someone come up and show me where I would need to make an edit? Thanks so much! I know that I can edit that and make it better. What was the second thing a superstar writer does? Yes, we need to check to see if I used two finger spaces. I did use spaces sometimes like right here between the words "is" and "yellow." I forgot my spaces between the words "my" and "chick." Can anyone else spy with your little eye a place where I forgot my spaces. Polishing partners are great detectives and help find places where their friends can edit their writing and make it better! Great job partners. Thanks for helping me! You are giving me lots of ideas to make my writing better.

Continue the same process as you discuss each star and look for samples of that convention applied in the writing sample. You can erase and fix the original sample right at that moment or you can use a clean sheet for your rewrite. Since we intentionally edit many errors during the first draft, I model rewriting on a clean sheet after discussing each star. Too much erasing can cause frustration for beginning writers.

Wow! Thanks so much polishing partners. I really want to be a six-star superstar writer so I am going to edit my work. I am going to write my story again and try to remember all of those important things we talked about. I am going to put my new paper right here next to the first one to help me remember how to make it better. Clip your second draft next to your first draft on the easel. Talk aloud as you edit each sentence. *I will start by fixing the first sentence and doing everything a superstar writer does. I need to start with a capital here. I need to leave two finger spaces, and I need to put a period at the end. I already did a nice job of using my word wall words in this sentence. I even sounded out my words carefully and wrote the letters for the beginning, middle, and ending sounds I heard. What do you think partners? Did I edit my writing in this first sentence to make it better? This is great. My sentence looks so much better. Thanks for helping me polish my work. I am excited to edit my next sentence.*

Continue the same process for the next two sentences. Talk aloud as you make corrections and engage the class in checking your work. It is always helpful to intentionally skip a correction and see if students will stop you and remind you to fix it. Kindergartners love correcting the teacher's "mistakes." At the end, be sure to discuss the illustration too. *Kindergartners, I can edit my illustration and make it better too. I need to make sure my writing and my illustration match. My words say the chick is yellow, but I forgot to color the chick in my first story. I can polish my illustration by making the chick yellow. Don't forget to check your illustrations when you edit and make them better too.*

Look at my edited work. (See Figure 7.7.) Read it to the class as you point to the words. *Partners, my second story is so amazing because you helped me polish it up. Do you think it is six-star superstar writing now? Why?* Encourage students to use the Superstar Writer Chart as a guide and find examples of each star in your writing. *Editing is so awesome because it makes our writing better. A kindergarten writing family helps one another edit. Thanks for helping me!*

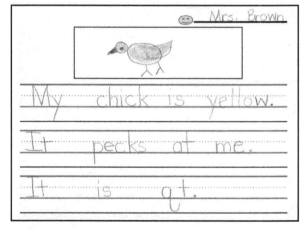

Figure 7.7 Teacher Sample: Second Draft of Chick Writing

Now you are ready to edit. I am going to give you a polishing partner. Remember, polishing partners help you look at the Superstar Writer Chart and see what stars you might be missing. Polishing partners use kind and

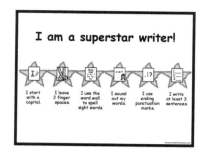

I am a superstar writer!

I start with a capital. I leave 2 finger spaces. I use the word wall to spell sight words. I sound out my words. I use ending punctuation marks. I write at least 3 sentences.

I can edit my writing to make it better.

Writing W.K. 5

I am a superstar speaker and a superstar writer.

Language L.K. 1

I can write my capital and lowercase letters.

Language L.K. 1a

I can share my ideas in complete sentences.

Language L.K. 1f

I can write sentences using capital letters, punctuation, and kindergarten spelling.

Language L.K. 2a-d

encouraging words to help each other. Partner one will read his or her writing first while partner two gives ideas on how to polish the writing. Then you will switch. You will need to take turns and be good listeners and careful detectives. When you are done talking about your writing, you can go to your table and write your second story with edits. Remember, first we are just talking about how to edit our work. We are looking at the Superstar Writer Chart and giving our friend ideas of how to polish up his or her story. When both of you have had a chance to talk about your stories, then you can go to your tables and write your edited story. Later, we will read our stories to our polishing partners. Who is ready to edit and become a six-star superstar writer? Awesome. When I put you in partners, get your chick story and find a quiet place to talk about editing. Let's go be polishing partners!

Pair up students. Be sure to assign partner one and partner two. Remind students to use the Superstar Writer Chart to guide their discussions. Be sure to have the chart displayed in many locations for easy reference. After students are partnered you will want to circulate and provide support. Editing is a skill that will need to be practiced routinely before kindergartners can do it independently.

Choose one student's work that shows growth and includes all six stars in the final draft. Have that student come up to the easel and share both stories in the Author's Chair. Encourage the student to talk about how his polishing partner helped him edit his story. Be sure to clip the first draft (Figure 7.8) and the second draft (Figure 7.9) to the easel.

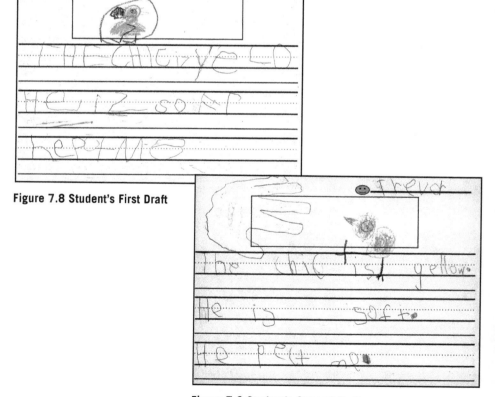

Figure 7.8 Student's First Draft

Figure 7.9 Student's Second Draft

Trevor, thanks for sharing your stories with us today. Your first story was very good, but I love the way you polished up your work and made it even better in your second story. Your editing is wonderful. Class, can you spy with your little eyes ways that Trevor edited his story? Who can tell us something that Trevor did to be a six-star superstar writer? Use Trevor's writing to talk about how to include all of the criteria on the Superstar Writer Chart. Reflecting while using a concrete sample is very powerful as it helps young writers truly see how to apply these important components in their writing. Guide students in looking for all six skills. *Let's give Trevor a cowboy for being a superstar writer. Yeehaw! Way to go Trevor! You're a six-star superstar writer!*

Engage students in the editing process repeatedly. You do not need to edit all of their work as that can be laborious. Pick at least one story per week to polish. It is effective if you model editing your work first and follow up with a student sharing his or her edits after working in polishing partners. This paints a picture of a kindergarten family where everyone helps one another become superstar writers.

When you feel that kindergartners can successfully edit their work with the support of a partner, it is time to encourage students to use an independent editing rubric. (See Figure 7.10.) Prepare a writing sample that only includes three of the star skills. Clip your writing and the rubric to the easel.

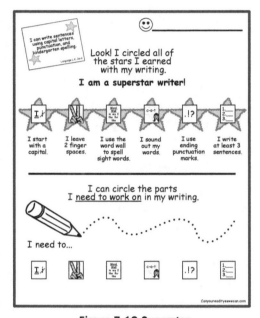

Figure 7.10 Superstar Writing Rubric, Full page available in Appendix

Kindergartners, this is a very special paper that can help us look closely at our writing and think about what we can edit to make it better. It is called a rubric. A rubric is a chart that we can use to see how many superstars we remembered to include in our work. I love this rubric because I get to write on it. First, I am going to write my name right here by the smiley face.

Look it has our learning goal at the top. Read the standard to students. *Let's grade my yak story using this rubric and see how many superstars I earned. This sentence says, "Look! I circled all of the stars I earned with my writing. I am a superstar writer!" This is so awesome. Will you help me see how many stars I earned?* Read your writing aloud and analyze your work for each star. Circle only the stars that you included in your work consistently.

Wow, I was a three-star superstar writer. I included capital letters. I wrote three sentences, and I used my kindergarten spelling. Three stars is a great start but I know that I can do better. I really want to be a six-star superstar writer. What do I still need to do to make my writing better? This rubric has a section at the bottom to help me set some goals on things I can do to edit my work. Draw attention to the bottom section of the Superstar Writing Rubric.

It says, "I can circle the parts I need to work on in my writing." Can you help me circle the right parts? Did I need to work on capitals? No, I did a great job at that, so I am skipping that picture. Did I need to work on two finger spaces? Yes! I better circle that picture. Continue this routine discussing each skill and deciding if it needs to be circled.

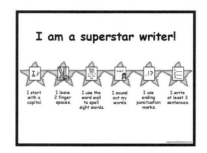

Thanks for helping me set some goals to make my writing better. We circled these three things that I need to polish up in my writing: two finger spacing, use the word wall, put in ending punctuation. Now I know exactly what I need to do to be a six-star superstar writer. Using this rubric helped me set goals to make my writing better.

Model writing an edited version of the story and be sure to demonstrate explicitly how to make the suggested changes. It is also crucial to help students understand that all writers edit. Your writing does not have to be perfect every time but a rubric can help you make it better. Read your second draft aloud and have students help you use the rubric to grade it. *Kindergartners, thanks for helping me use this rubric to make my work better. I love the way it helps me grade my work to see how many stars I earned. But the best part is how it helps me circle goals of how to make my work better. It really made me think about my work. Now I am a six-star superstar writer. I get to make six stars at the top of my paper. Let's give my writing some fireworks!*

Now it is your turn to use the special rubric. Do you remember your yak writing from yesterday? We will use the rubric to make your yak writing even better. Since it is your first time using a rubric, I thought we could do it together. You will get to come up to my desk and we can talk about your writing together. That is called a conference.

I am excited to have a writing conference with each of you. During our conference we will circle all of the superstars at the top of your rubric that you earned. Then at the bottom we will circle the goals of things you need to edit. When we are done conferencing, you will get to polish up your work using your rubric goals. If you remember to include everything on the rubric, you can put six stars on your paper for being a six-star superstar writer! Who's a superstar writer? Yes, you are all superstar writers!

Using a rubric will help students become reflective about their own writing. Students who can self-assess their work become confident and effective writers. The rubric will need to be used many times during whole class and followed up with a teacher conference before kindergartners can be expected to use it independently. Stapling the rubric to the first draft and then stapling the second draft to the top really helps students feel a sense of pride and accomplishment when they see their writing progress. This could be shared at home too. Parents benefit from seeing how the editing process works and being reminded of the important writing goals focused on in the classroom.

Using a rubric also provides a visual anchor for students to use when writing. The thought of earning more stars with every component included is motivating to young writers. The confidence they gain each time they concretely see that they can be a superstar writer is contagious. Don't forget the celebrating. High five your students after they edit, and tell them how proud you are of their six-star superstar writing. Your positive feedback is priceless!

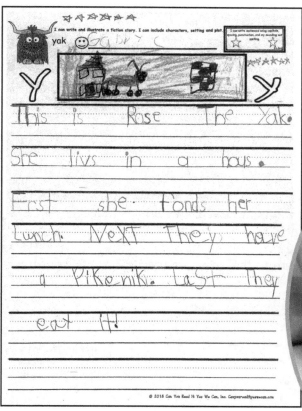

This is a student's six-star edited yak writing. Note her six stars at the top.

These kindergartners wrote and then performed a play.

Center/Small Group Practice

Use these activities to engage students in practicing Common Core Writing and Language Standards.

- **Writing Centers:**
  - **Post Office**
  - **Greeting Card Center**
  - **Journalism Center**
  - **Construction Center**
  - **Wordless Books Center:** Have students use wordless books to write captions.
  - **Drama Center:** Encourage students to write and perform plays.

- **Writing Games:**
  - **How Many Words Can You Write in 2 and 5 minutes?**
  - **Message in a Bottle:** Invite students to grab 3–5 words to create a sentence.
  - **Silly Sentences Game (A Dorling Kindersley game)**

- **Making Class Books:** Have a variety of writing materials available, including blank pages stapled together for book making.

Independent Practice

Use these activities to engage students in practicing the Common Core Writing and Language Standards.

- **Prompt Writing**
- **Journal Writing:** Engage students to write about math, science, and so on.
- **Recipe Writing**
- **Dialogue Writing:** Encourage students to write in talk bubbles.
- **Experiential Writing**
- **Silly Story Writing**
- **Reading and Writing the Room**
- **Research Writing**
- **Song Writing**
- **Poetry Writing**
- **Book Report Writing**
- **Letter Writing:** Have students write letters for a variety of audiences.
- **ABC Book Writing**
- **Fiction and Nonfiction Writing**
- **All About Me Poster Writing**
- **Advertisement Writing**
- **Sign Writing**
- **Scientist Diagrams and Label Writing**
- **Filmstrip Retelling Writing**
- **Travel Brochure Writing**

Parent Connections

- **Parent Night:** Model for parents how to reinforce learning how to write at home. Give parents key phrases like "superstar writer" to connect the learning and excitement of writing at home. Also explain developmental spelling in kindergarten writing.

- **Parent Letter:** Create a parent newsletter to send home as you teach writing in the classroom. Parents are usually willing to practice but they do not always know what to do. Provide them with ideas to support their emergent writers and take them to the next level on the writing continuum. (See Figure 7.11.)

Figure 7.11 Writing Parent Newsletter Full pages available in Appendix

Technology Tips

Use these activities to help students practice the Common Core Writing and Language Standards.

- **Writing on the Computer:** Use programs like Kid Pix, Microsoft Paint, and PowerPoint for a variety of writing activities. For example, you could use these programs to encourage kindergartners to write a story and illustrate it or write a fact about something he or she learned in the classroom and illustrate the fun fact.

- **Pencil Power of the App:** Search for apps that will support writers at all levels. Some apps encourage the development of fine motor skills and others will engage students in the process of writing like brainstorming, organizing, and so on.

- **Grab the Glitz:** Use a variety of technology tools to create more interesting final products, such as slideshow animations, graphics, and so on.

- **Online Buddies:** Encourage students to write to online pen pals, famous authors, other kindergarten classrooms, and so on.

- **Bloggers Bash:** Create a kindergarten classroom blog or website to show student writing and projects.

Children's Books for Teaching Writing

Great Books for Teaching the Art of Writing

For brainstorming and the art of writing
Rocket Writes a Story by Tad Hills, published by Random House

For letter writing
Dear Peter Rabbit by Alma Flor Ada, published by Aladdin
I Wanna Iguana by Karen Kaufman Orloff, published by Putnam

For persuasive writing
Don't Let the Pigeon Stay Up Late! by Mo Willems, published by Hyperion Books

For expository writing
Look What I Did With a Leaf! by Morteza E. Sohi, published by Walker Publishing Company

For narrative writing
The True Story of the 3 Little Pigs by Jon Scieszka, published by Puffin

Great Books for Teaching the Conventions of Writing
Word Fun series, published by Capstone

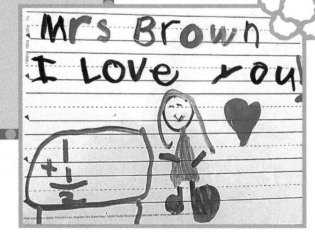

Writing Assessments

- Use the ELA Assessment Checklist: Writing Standards while students are working independently or engaged at literacy centers. (See Figure 7.12.)

- Use the Language ELA Assessment Checklist: Language Standards while students are working independently or engaged at literacy centers. (See Figure 7.13.)

- Use a Superstar Writing Rubric while students are working independently or engaged at literacy centers. (See Figure 7.14.)

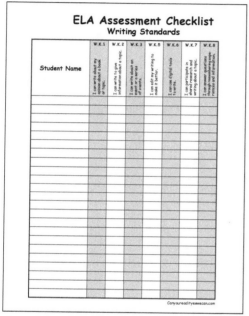

Figure 7.12 ELA Assessment Checklist: Writing Standards, Full page available in Appendix

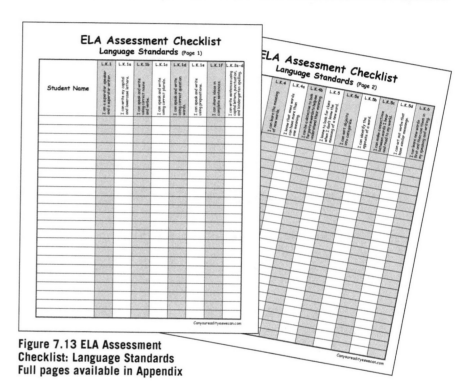

Figure 7.13 ELA Assessment Checklist: Language Standards Full pages available in Appendix

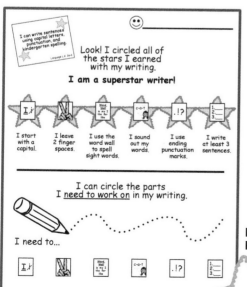

Figure 7.14 Superstar Writing Rubric, Full page available in Appendix

CHAPTER 8

WHO'S A SUPERSTAR SPEAKER AND LISTENER? Strategies for Teaching Speaking and Listening (SL.K)

Communication is at the heart of everything we do in life. It doesn't matter if you are a toddler or a grandparent; you interact with others in a multitude of ways each day. It is a simple fact that we all speak and listen more than we do anything else in life. Communication is also the cornerstone of learning.

Kindergartners need to successfully use speaking and listening to explore new ideas and connect to old experiences. Conversation is the critical underpinning of all learning, as talk is the foundation that cements prior knowledge and stimulates the construction of new thinking. NAEYC (2009) suggests, "To enhance children's conceptual understanding, teachers use various strategies, including intensive interview and conversation, that encourage children to reflect on and 'revisit' their experiences." When young children talk, it exposes their thoughts, providing a window of insight for themselves and others.

Prior to entering kindergarten, most children spend a significant amount of time talking. Young learners are innately egocentric and skilled at sharing their ideas but not patient enough to be attentive listeners. Yet when they begin school, students are typically required to listen for extended periods of time.

As a well-intentioned teacher, I spent countless hours teaching my students to be focused listeners. I became an expert at using speaking and listening as classroom management tools. I looked at unstructured "talk" as an opportunity for chaos and potential loss of control. I feared what could happen if students actually engaged in and acted upon conversations they might have with one another. I wondered if I opened the floodgates of social interaction, how would I ever regain control of their attention? Instead, I tightly held onto the reins of talk by using it to check for learning rather than develop thinking. I created a whole group teaching routine of teacher interrogation instead of class conversation. First, I asked a question. Next, a student raised his or her hand and answered. Then, I provided confirmation that the answer was correct. If it wasn't correct, I steered the student to state the targeted response. I used this pattern of instruction as an instrument to "cover" curriculum when instead I should have been inspiring my students to "discover" new learning.

Open wide the window of insight for your students. Don't be afraid to encourage classroom conversations. Let your students' voices roar and their minds ignite! Take back some precious moments to help students learn how to talk in a collaborative classroom. Grant the gift of time: time to talk, time to listen, time to interact, and time to truly learn!

Igniting the Interaction-Infused Environment

Learners thrive in classrooms where speaking and listening are emphasized. Kindergartners need to feel safe talking about what they see, feel, hear, and think. The classroom needs to be a place where ideas are shared freely and a variety of responses are celebrated. Excitement and ownership are born from encouraged expression. Talk is especially powerful when young children use it to make their ideas understood by others. Discussion requires two-way conversations that nurture new thoughts and respect for other ideas. If students are solely required to repeat rote responses, they are only memorizing answers. When peers challenge one another in classroom conversations, kindergartners are engaged in higher-level thinking like clarifying and explaining. A community of learners that collaborates to describe their thoughts fosters a sense of wonder and empowerment for all learners.

Cultivate a climate of collaborative conversation. When talk becomes a platform of priority, classrooms are transformed into dynamic learning environments. All students are instantly engaged at one time and eager to chat about the day's learning targets. This vibrant learning atmosphere doesn't just happen by chance. Parameters must be set so students understand that classroom discussions are defined by purposeful and productive talk that helps us learn. Attitudes of respect for one another and eagerness to learn must also be carefully developed.

In an interactive classroom, going to school is no longer a chore but a desired destination. Excitement exudes from students and ownership unfolds as they feel inspired to share their thoughts. Children anxiously await discussing ideas with one another and can clearly follow classroom expectations as they banter back and forth. Collaborative conversations become a catalyst for learning new content while simultaneously improving emotional and social skills. Talk facilitates well-rounded learners.

Children learn about content as they learn about one another. Infuse opportunities to talk across all instructional settings within your kindergarten day. Spark speaking and listening during whole group read-alouds, small group reading and writing activities, center work, partner activities, and so on. Encourage your students to be detectives and talk about likenesses and differences they see in the world around them. Coach your class to compare and contrast, explain and evaluate, and clarify and critique. Wake up the wonder of learning in your students by inviting interaction, fueling fascination, kindling curiosity, promoting problem-solving, inspiring investigation, and arousing reflection.

The Art of Speaking and Listening in the Classroom

Teaching speaking and listening is more like an art rather than a prearranged lesson plan. Helping children become effective communicators requires modeling, shaping, and reflecting. You can't follow a scripted plan but instead respond to the teachable moment. Provide impromptu instruction that is highly responsive to the needs and interests of the students sitting right in front of you. Don't be afraid to let day-to-day discussions illuminate your teaching environment and carry your kindergartners to new levels of learning. Capitalize on the spontaneous conversations that unfold in the classroom to shape superstar speakers and listeners.

Lev Vygotsky underscores the importance of interaction in the classroom in his theory, the zone of proximal development. When students are

engaged in conversations with a more capable peer they have the opportunity to learn from that peer. Talking with a more advanced friend can lead to new levels of learning that are not possible when students learn in isolation. It doesn't matter if you call it a shoulder partner, a turn-and-talk, a think-pair-share, or a buddy talk—it is important that you engage students in partner conversations. The listening peer will benefit from hearing the thinking of others. The speaking peer will benefit from using language to clarify his or her thoughts. These are skills that kindergartners would not develop if they had not been engaged in interaction. You can assign turn and talk buddies or let children choose their partners. You know what is most effective for your learners.

Kindergartners do not come to school naturally knowing how to engage in a turn and talk. Use a gradual release method of instruction to develop superstar speakers and listeners. Modeling appropriate listening and speaking behaviors is crucial to supply a concrete point of reference. First, model being a superstar listener who is sensitive and actively interested in the speaker's thoughts. Asking follow-up questions and praising the speaker's ideas is a great way to paint a picture of a good listener. Next, model being a superstar speaker by staying on topic and looking at your audience when conveying a message. Then, provide many opportunities for guided practice. Ask two student volunteers to model being superstar listeners and speakers. Focus on how to take turns and have a conversation with multiple exchanges. Encourage classmates to provide feedback to the volunteers. Last, allow students to practice having collaborative conversations with a partner. Be sure to set a purpose for learning like, "Turn to your partner and share three things that you like about spring." Also, don't forget to tell them what you want them to do to signify they are done sharing. Having students turn back to the front and put their hands in their laps works well. Monitor and provide feedback as needed. Clarify any misunderstandings and praise appropriate speaking and listening. Look for two or three excellent speaking and listening partners that can later share and serve as models for the class. This turn-and-talk routine can be applied throughout the kindergarten day in multiple content areas. Once students know how to turn to a friend and share, the strategy can be used effectively in any lesson.

Speaking and Listening Everywhere

Talk to parents on how to support their kindergartners in being superstar speakers and listeners. Parents appreciate when you share ideas at curriculum night or in newsletters. We typically help parents support reading and writing at home but often neglect giving tips about talking. Speaking and listening are powerful skills that can certainly be practiced at home. Once students know the rules of speaking and listening engagement, they can be applied anywhere. Your parents will also quickly notice what attentive listeners their children have become at home too!

The Common Core Standards have heightened the importance of speaking and listening. Performance-based assessment has become an everyday occurrence in education. The days of only paper and pencil tests are diminishing. Students now are expected to be able to effectively demonstrate and explain their thinking through presentations and projects. Speaking and listening are critical skills used to show mastery in learning and therefore need to be practiced across all content areas.

Kindergarten is the gateway to learning, so we must help our students become experts at showing and telling what they know. Young children should view the classroom as their stage: a place where they can share and shine! Providing opportunities for open-ended, project-based learning allows for increased interaction. Here are just a few ideas:

• Have your students make and present videos about their favorite animal or color.

• Engage students in role-playing a meteorologist who communicates the current weather forecasts.

- Inspire kindergartners to write and present a play persuading others to be a good friend.

- Invite students to enlighten the class on how they solved a difficult math problem.

- Create a coat stand of colorful words. Ask students to hang new vocabulary words on the coat stand as they describe their meaning.

Activities that encourage collaborative conversations not only actively engage the entire class simultaneously, but also promote the practice of both expressive and receptive language. Project-based learning is particularly effective because it allows students to use speaking and listening skills in purposeful ways and teachers to authentically assess speaking and listening skills at the same time.

These boys are engaged in a collaborative conversation comparing and contrasting their crazy caps.

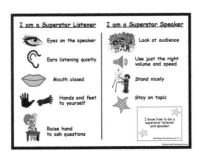

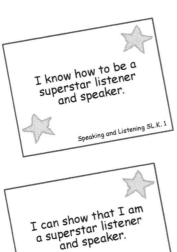

I know how to be a superstar listener and speaker.

Speaking and Listening SL.K.1

I can show that I am a superstar listener and speaker.

Speaking and Listening SL.K.1a

I take turns listening and speaking.

Speaking and Listening SL.K.1b

I can be a superstar speaker.

Speaking and Listening SL.K.6

You should intentionally plan for incorporating multiple standards into a lesson. In Lesson 1, a speaking and listening lesson can be used to bundle standards SL.K.1, SL.K.1a, SL.K.1b, and SL.K.6. Also, since reading, foundational skills, writing, speaking, and listening are mutually reinforcing skills, several of these strand areas are naturally integrated in the lesson.

Lesson 1

Who's a Superstar Speaker and Listener?

The poster is published by www.canyoureadityeswecan.com

For this lesson, we are focusing on introducing how to be a superstar listener and speaker. You could apply this speaking and listening routine to any content area.

Set the stage for standards learning. Begin the lesson by referring to the Let's Learn! wall and saying, *Kindergartners, look at the skills we are going to practice today.* Instill focus and enthusiasm for speaking and listening by having your students recite the day's posted learning targets. Continue with, *Why do you think we need to learn these skills?* Encourage students to respond with, *Because that is what good speakers and listeners need to do.* Cement the commitment of the class to learning by excitedly asking, *Who's a superstar learner?* Pump them up to respond, "I'm a superstar learner!" Last, confirm their pledge by saying, *Yes, you are superstars! I am so proud of you. Now, let's learn.*

Gather kindergartners in the shared area. *Boys and girls do you remember the story* Listen, Buddy *by Helen Lester? What lesson did Buddy learn?* Accept all responses and encourage students to remember that Buddy could have been a better listener. *Buddy got in a lot of trouble when he didn't listen carefully. We want to be good listeners in kindergarten. Being a good listener takes lots of practice. What do you think a good listener does? Turn to a friend and share your thoughts.* Encourage students to discuss in partners what good listeners do. Provide feedback as needed. Discuss ideas as a whole group.

Kindergartners, I made you a very special poster. It will help us be a family of superstar speakers and listeners. (See Figure 8.1.) *When we talk to one another we have two different jobs that we need to do. Sometimes we need to be the speaker and sometimes we need to be the listener. This poster helps us remember how to do both jobs.*

Let's look at this side of the poster first. Point to the left side of the poster and engage students in dialogue about listening. *This side of the poster shows us how to be great listeners. What do you think this picture of an eye is showing us about being a good listener?* Encourage students to conclude that good listeners keep their eyes on the speaker. *Wow! Great job, friends! You are right. To be a good listener you need to keep your eyes on the speaker. Who is speaking right now? Yes, I am. If you're being good* listeners, where should your eyes be? Awesome job, superstar listeners. I can see that you all have your eyes looking at me. Give yourselves some fireworks.

Boys and girls, who can tell me what you think the picture of the ear is telling us to do? Encourage students to conclude that good listeners keep their ears open and listen quietly to the speaker. Super job, kindergartners! You are right. To be a good listener you need to keep your ears open and listen quietly to the speaker.

Kindergartners, let's look at the next picture on our poster. It is a mouth. What could this picture be telling us about

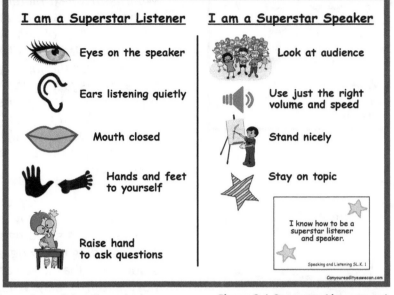

Figure 8.1 Superstar Listener and Speaker Poster available in color at www.canyoureadityeswecan.com Full page available in the Appendix

being a good listener? When I say "go," turn to a friend and share your ideas. Turn back to the front with your hands in your lap when you have both shared. Go! Encourage partners to discuss the importance of keeping their mouths closed to be good listeners. Provide feedback as needed. Discuss ideas as a whole group. Kindergartners, you are right. This picture shows us that good listeners keep their mouths quiet. Why do you think that is important? Take several responses. Yes, if we all talked at the same time no one would be able to be heard. We have to remember, if it is our turn to be the listener, then we shouldn't be talking.

Repeat the same routine with the next two pictures on the listener side of the poster. Be sure to engage students in dialogue and collaborative conversations to help them construct meaning from the poster.

Kindergartners, you are such superstar listeners. I bet you can use this poster to help you tell a friend about the five things that a superstar listener does. Remember to take turns being the speaker and listener. You will need to decide who will be the speaker first and who will be the listener first. When I say "go," share your ideas with a friend. Turn back to the front with your hands in your lap when you have both shared. Go! Monitor conversations and provide feedback when needed. Choose a partner pair to share their discussion with the group.

You are awesome listeners! I am so proud of you. Let's look at the other side of our poster and learn how to be superstar speakers now. Look at this picture. Who can describe what you see? Facilitate a discussion either in whole group or in partners about how a good speaker looks at their audience. You will need to discuss what an audience is and why a speaker is better understood when looking at the audience. This is a good opportunity to model not looking at your audience as it will spark correction from your students. Boys and girls, tell me if I am being a good speaker. You are my audience, but I am looking at the ceiling, the walls, and my sparkly pink nail polish. What am I doing wrong? Oh no! I forgot to look at you: my audience. Thanks for reminding me that a good speaker always looks at his or her audience.

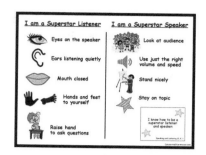

I know how to be a superstar listener and speaker.

Speaking and Listening SL.K. 1

I can show that I am a superstar listener and speaker.

Speaking and Listening SL.K. 1a

I take turns listening and speaking.

Speaking and Listening SL.K. 1b

I can be a superstar speaker.

Speaking and Listening SL.K. 6

What is this next picture on our poster? Have you ever seen one of these before? It is a volume button that reminds us to use just the right voice when we talk to others. We don't want to talk too loud or too soft or too fast or too slow. It is just like Goldilocks and the Three Bears. *Goldilocks was searching for the just right chair, porridge, and bed. We want to find the voice that is just right.* Demonstrate a variety of inappropriate and appropriate voices. Have your students give you a thumbs-up if it is just right or thumbs-down if it is not just right. *Fantastic job, kindergartners! You will know how to use exactly the right voice when you are a superstar speaker. Your listeners will understand everything you say when you use your just right voice.*

Let's look at the next picture on our poster. It is a boy standing by an easel. What is he doing? Why is this important? Encourage students to conclude that the boy is standing nicely when he speaks to his audience. *Tell me if I am standing nicely right now.* Turn backward. Even try spinning to inspire student feedback. *You are so smart. I can't be a superstar speaker if I am not standing nicely. When I am moving all around I can't be understood. I need to stand nicely when I speak. Standing nicely means facing my audience and standing still. Does anyone want to come up and model being a superstar speaker by standing nicely?* Take several volunteers to demonstrate standing nicely and not so nicely. *That was so fun. I can definitely tell when someone is standing nicely and ready to be a superstar speaker.*

Do you spy with your little eye the star next? The star tells us that this picture is very important. It tells us that to be a superstar speaker we must always stay on topic. What does topic mean? Engage students in discussing the concept of a main topic. Use a recent story as a concrete example. *Remember the book we read about going to school? Every page was about a different way we could go to school. The pages were all connected by one main idea or main topic. That main topic was school. Was our book about food? No. Was our book about dogs? No. The main topic that connected our book was school. When we are superstar speakers, the words we choose have to be connected by a main topic too. If we are speaking about the topic of colors, we would want to only share ideas about our favorite colors. We would talk only about colors and not about other things. Listen to my story. Raise your hand when you know the main topic of my story. Remember, the main topic is the idea that connects all my other ideas together.* Tell a story with three connected sentences about dogs. *Yes, you are right. My main topic was about dogs. All of my ideas were connected by the topic of dogs. Give yourselves a cowboy. Yeehaw!*

Now it is your turn to practice staying on topic. Your topic is pizza. When I say "go," stay on topic and share with your partner about pizza. Remember to take turns being the speaker and being the listener. Turn back to the front with your hands in your lap when you have both shared. Go! Facilitate collaborative conversations that stay on topic, and provide feedback as needed. Choose two to three partner pairs to share their ideas with the group.

Let's review everything a good superstar speaker does. Use our special poster and tell your friend how to be a good speaker. When I say "go," share your thoughts. Turn back to the front with your hands in your lap when you have both shared. Go! Facilitate collaborative conversations that stay on topic, and provide feedback as needed. Choose one partner pair to share with the group. Make sure they are following the guidelines of a good speaker. *Yes, kindergartners! Good speakers do four important things. Let's say them together as I point on the poster.* Point to each picture as the class choral reads.

Wow! I am so proud of you. You know what to do to be a superstar speaker and listener. Give yourselves a round of applause. I am going to hang up this poster around the room so that you can look at it whenever you are talking with a friend, a teacher, or even to the whole class. I am excited to watch you be a kindergarten family of superstar speakers and listeners. I love it when we learn by sharing ideas with one another. You are amazing kindergartners!

You should intentionally plan for incorporating multiple standards into a lesson. In Lesson 2, a speaking and listening lesson can be used to bundle standards SL.K.1a, SL.K.1b, SL.K.3, SL.K.4, SL.K.5, SL.K.6, and L.K.1. Also, since reading, foundational skills, writing, speaking, and listening are mutually reinforcing skills, several of these standard strand areas are naturally integrated in the lesson.

Lesson 2

All About Me: September Sight Word Bundle

Published by www.canyoureadityeswecan.com

For this lesson, we focus on all about me. You could apply this speaking and listening routine to any content area.

Set the stage for standards learning. Begin the lesson by referring to the Let's Learn! wall and saying, *Kindergartners, look at the skills we are going to practice today.* Instill focus and enthusiasm for speaking and listening by having your students recite the day's posted learning targets. Continue with, *Why do you think we need to learn these skills?* Encourage students to respond with, "Because that is what good speakers and listeners need to do." Cement the commitment of the class to learning by excitedly asking, *Who's a superstar learner?* Pump them up to respond "I'm a superstar learner!" Last, confirm their pledge by saying, *Yes, you are superstars! I am so proud of you. Now, let's learn.*

Gather kindergartners in the shared area. *Boys and girls do you remember when we read the books,* I Like Me *by Nancy Carlson and* I Like Myself *by Karen Beaumont?* Show the front covers of several all about me books that you recently read in class. *What was the main topic that connected these books? That's right! These are all about me books. They tell details all about the main character in the book. Today our main topic is going to be all about me too. We are going to talk and write all about us! When we share our ideas, we will need to remember to be superstar listeners and speakers. Let's look at our special poster to help us remember what superstar listeners and speakers do.* Review the Superstar Listener and Speaker Poster.

There is only one special you. No one else is exactly like you. Look around the room—we are all different. You have your own special skin, eyes, hair, family, and favorite things. Since we are a kindergarten family, we should get to know each other better. Let's make All About Me *books. We can write interesting things about ourselves in our books. Then we can be superstar listeners and speakers and share our books so that everyone in our learning family can get to know us better. I am very excited to learn new things about all of you.*

Let's practice by making a book together. Can you help me make an All About Me *book?* Place your teacher *All About Me Book* (see Figure 8.2) on the easel with just the front cover showing. Encourage students to read the title with you. All About Me *By. What should I write here? Yes I am the author of this book, so I need to write my name here.* Model writing your name on the front cover. *What is the main topic of this book? Yes it is all about me, Mrs. Brown. When you make your book it will be all about you. Here is a circle so that I can add my picture to the front cover. I am going to make it look just like me. I am drawing and coloring my hair, eyes, and skin. Now the front cover looks like me!*

Figure 8.2 *All About Me Book* **September Sight Word Bundle available in color at www.canyoureadityeswecan.com**

When I say "go," I want you to turn to a friend and share with your friend how you will make the front cover look like you. Make sure you describe details about the color of your hair, skin, eyes, and everything else! Also, don't forget to decide who will be the speaker first and who will be the listener first. Then take turns. When you have both finished sharing, show me by turning to the front and putting your hands in your lap. Ready to share what you look like, superstar listeners and speakers? Go! Monitor and provide feedback. Celebrate descriptive details and a variety of responses.

Let's turn the page and see what interesting fact about me we are going to write about first. I see a picture of a house. What do you think this sentence might say? Let's read it together. Read and point to the words. *Nice reading, friends!*

Since sight word practice is embedded in this book, you will want to discuss the word "is." *There is a special word that we are going to practice today. It is dotted. Can you read it? Yes, it is the word "is." On every page of this book, we are going to write the word "is." Let's read this page*

together one more time. *This is my house. What do you think I should draw here? Yes, since the words tell us about a house, my illustration has to match. I need to draw my house with lots of great details in the box. My house is gray with six windows, black shutters, and a black door. While I am drawing my house, I want you to turn to a friend and talk about where you live and describe with details what you are going to draw on this page. Be sure to take turns. Turn back to the front with your hands in your lap when you have both shared. Go!* Monitor and provide feedback. Celebrate descriptive details and a variety of responses.

Continue this routine for each page of the book. Use your teacher book for modeling. Be sure to allow time for talking about each page, as talk is the rehearsal for writing. Students need to talk to brainstorm their ideas so that they will be ready to write their own books. You can use turn and talks or whole class discussions. Refer back to the Superstar Listener and Speaker Poster often and celebrate when students are demonstrating those skills.

Kindergartners, thanks for helping me make this book all about me. I am really proud of it because it tells interesting things about me. I want to be a superstar speaker now and share it with you. Can you help me remember what a superstar speaker does? Let's look at our poster. Facilitate a discussion about being a superstar speaker. *Thanks for helping me remember what a great speaker does. When I read my book to you I will try to remember to look at my audience, use just the right voice, stand nicely, and stay on topic. Now if I am the speaker, what will you all be doing? Yes, you will be the listeners. Do you remember what superstar listeners do? Let's look at our poster.* Facilitate a discussion about being a superstar listener. *When I am being a superstar speaker and reading my book, you will need to be superstar listeners. Are you ready, superstar listeners? I want to share my book.*

Read your book, stopping to periodically ask if you are being a superstar speaker. Try speaking too fast or too soft or not looking at your audience. See if your students will catch you and give you helpful feedback.

Kindergartners, thanks for helping me be a superstar speaker when I shared my book. You were amazing listeners too. It is fun to share interesting facts. Now it is your turn to make an All About Me Book. *You are ready because you have already shared with a friend your great ideas to put on each page. Don't forget to use lots of detail. When you are finished, we will read our books to two friends. Reading our books to friends lets us practice being superstar speakers and listeners. I can't wait to see your fabulous* All About Me Books! (See Figure 8.3.)

Figure 8.3 *All About Me Book Student Sample*

Monitor and provide feedback as students work on their *All About Me Books.* Be sure to have them read their books to two friends in the classroom. You can ask students to read to you too. This will give you an authentic opportunity to assess their reading, writing, speaking, and listening skills. Praise students for being amazing workers. Celebrate all of the learning that has taken place.

Kindergartners, give yourselves a cowboy! Yeehaw! Your All About Me Books *were fantastic. I love the way you were superstar listeners and speakers when you shared them with one another. Make sure you read your book to your family at home. They will be so proud of you too! You are awesome learners!*

These kindergartners are being superstar speakers and listeners.

Center/Small Group Practice

Use these activities to engage students in practicing Speaking and Listening and Language Standards.

- **Puppet Theater:** Have children write and perform puppet shows re-enacting their favorite stories or characters.

- **Reader's Theater:** Have children perform Reader's Theaters stories and plays. Encourage them to do it for multiple audiences.

- **Interview a Friend Center:** Supply questionnaires on clipboards. Have students interview each other and then present their findings.

- **Explain a Block Design Center:** Put out Legos, Connectagons, pattern blocks, Lincoln Logs, and so on and have students create a structure and draw it. Inspire students to present their drawings, explaining the materials used and discussing the construction.

- **All About Me Poster Presentation Station:** Have parents send in pictures of their child or have children draw significant moments in their lives. Set out a variety of materials, including poster boards. Have the students create All About Me posters and present them to class, parents, grandparents, the principal, and so on.

- **Games:** Play games that emphasize taking turns, listening to others, and collaborating.

- **Read to a Friend:** Have students read books or stories they create in class or those they like to a friend.

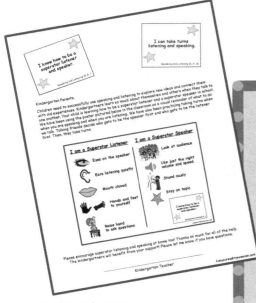

Figure 8.4 Speaking and
Listening Parent Newsletter
Full page available in Appendix

Parent Connections

- **Parent Night:** Model for parents how to reinforce speaking and listening at home. Give parents key phrases like "superstar listener" to connect the learning at home. Also explain to parents the importance of new vocabulary and discussing new words with their kindergartners when they read.

- **Parent Letter:** Send home a parent newsletter as you introduce speaking and listening rules in the classroom. Parents are willing to practice but they do not always know what to do. Provide them with ideas to encourage their kindergartners to be confident speakers and engaged listeners. (See Figure 8.4.)

Technology Tips

Use these activities to engage students in practicing Speaking and Listening and Language Standards.

- **Kindergarten Broadcast Station:** Have a parent helper or a community member help students videotape presentations about classroom events and happenings.
- **Multimedia Center:** Create a center where students can go to make slide shows and movies to present to the class.
- **Technology Supplies:** Supply microphones, tape recorders, and video recorders like flip cameras. Kindergartners will love using new technology to make presentations.

Children's Books for Teaching Speaking, Listening, and Language

Duck Rabbit! by Amy Krouse Rosenthal and Tom Lichtenheld, published by Chronicle Books

How to Lose All Your Friends by Nancy Carlson, published by Puffin

I Am a Leader by Sarah L. Schuette, published by Capstone

I Am Respectful by Sarah L. Schuette, published by Capstone

Listen, Buddy by Helen Lester, published by HMH Books for Young Readers

Oral Language: Speaking and Listening in the Classroom set, published by Capstone

Rules of the Wild: An Unruly Book of Manners by Bridget Levin, published by Chronicle Books

Sight Word bundles, published by www.canyoureadityeswecan.com

The Big Orange Splot by Daniel Manus Pinkwater, published by Scholastic

Words Are Not for Hurting by Elizabeth Verdick, published by Free Spirit Publishing

Wordless Books that Encourage Language Development

Pancakes for Breakfast by Tomie dePaola, published by HMH Books for Young Readers

The Snowman by Raymond Briggs, published by Random House

Tuesday by David Wiesner, published by HMH Books for Young Readers

You're a Good Dog, Carl by Alexandra Day, published by Aladdin

Zoom by Istvan Banyai, published by Penguin Group

Speaking and Listening and Language Assessments

- Use the ELA Assessment Checklist: Speaking and Listening Standards while students are working independently or engaged at literacy centers. (See Figure 8.5.)

- Use the ELA Assessment Checklist: Language Standards while students are working independently or engaged at literacy centers. (See Figure 8.6.)

- Use anecdotal records and notes while students are working independently or engaged in the classroom. You can place these notes in portfolios or digital portfolios.

ELA Assessment Checklist
Speaking and Listening Standards

Student Name	SL.K.1	SL.K.1a	SL.K.1b	SL.K.2	SL.K.3	SL.K.4	SL.K.5	SL.K.6

Canyoureadityeswecan.com

Figure 8.5 ELA Assessment Checklist: Speaking and Listening Standards
Full page available in Appendix

ELA Assessment Checklist
Language Standards (Page 1)

Student Name	L.K.1	L.K.1a	L.K.1b	L.K.1c	L.K.1d	L.K.1e	L.K.1f	L.K.2a-d

Canyoureadityeswecan.com

Figure 8.6 ELA Assessment Checklist: Language Standards
Full page available in Appendix

CHAPTER 9

WHO'S A SUPERSTAR TEACHER?
You're a Superstar Teacher!

Teaching is arguably one of the most difficult professions that exist. Daily, we are faced with new learning curves as our job description changes. Children's needs transform. New curriculum is added. Parent concerns emerge. Additional assessments are required. Learning standards heighten. No matter how hard we try, teachers can never be completely prepared nor can teaching ever be consistently perfect. There is no miraculous instructional strategy that can be effective for all students at all moments. The magic is in our approach as we face ever-changing challenges.

We must adorn ourselves with the armor of an affirmative attitude. Embracing an optimistic outlook will help us welcome each day with the energy and commitment required to do our very best. Don't let the stress of the daily demands defeat you. Find that inner voice that motivates you to persevere. Just like your students, when you put forth your best effort, you are a superstar. Who's a superstar teacher? Remember, you're a superstar teacher!

Your enthusiasm will be contagious. Kindergartners will be excited to learn new things if you are excited to teach and learn alongside them. Cultivate a dynamic learning environment where students are thrilled to discover and acquire new knowledge. Excitedly and intentionally immerse standards in daily routines and activities in an effort to create a vibrant Common Core-focused classroom.

Imagine yourself as a chef with the task of cooking up an extraordinary classroom. First, you need to exude all of the characteristics of a great culinary artist. Be passionate about your students like a chef is passionate about food. Be creative in your instructional approaches just as a chef is always trying something new. Be observant. Successful cooks pay attention to detail. Teaching, like cooking, is an art where every ingredient added has a specific role. New things put in the pot change the taste of the dish, so you must be conscious of how your children are reacting to new instruction. Be responsive and decisive. An awesome chef has to be able to analyze problems and make timely decisions to prepare the most delicious dishes. Make decisions daily based on your students' needs. Be a master multitasker. An effective cook juggles multiple pans at once to produce the perfect meal. Be aware of everything happening in the classroom and orchestrate an on-task environment. Commit to quality. A top chef seeks out ways to deliver the best product possible. Be relentless. Have high expectations for your students. Be a team player. Just like a chef, we can't do it by ourselves. Forge partnerships with others and work together! Most importantly, be reflective. Amazing cooks seek out feedback and strive to make their dishes better each time they cook. Successful teaching requires daily reflection and repeated powerful practice.

Now it is time to cook up a Common Core classroom! Begin with a developmentally appropriate atmosphere by pouring in a gallon of enthusiastic attitude and two liters of print-rich environment. Next, add three heaping cups of routines including those that display, communicate, and integrate the Common Core Standards. Mix these routines carefully into the enthusiastic environment to create a kindergarten family of focused learners. Blend in a tablespoon each of collaborative conversations, authentic literacy explorations, respect, and higher-level thinking to create well-rounded learners. Drop in a dollop of humor with a pinch of play. Sprinkle generous amounts of praise and confidence over the entire mixture to make your kindergartners sparkle with empowerment. Spread into a pan coated with encouragement and acceptance. Bake for 180 days but monitor carefully as it cooks. Check in on the students frequently to authentically assess the progress of your masterpiece. Saturate with celebration and scaffold support as needed. Serve with a powerful plate of parent partnerships. Bon appétit!

Don't let the intensive demands of the Common Core Standards deter you from doing what you have always done for your students. Continue to help each and every child make progress in his or her journey of lifelong learning. Cook up a recipe of success that guides your students to meet the rigorous demands of the standards and empowers them to feel like they can do anything! Be a superstar teacher. Turn the challenge of the Common Core Standards into a triumph for your kindergartners!

References

A Joint Position Statement of the International Reading Association and the National Association for the Education of Young Children. 1998. "Learning to Read and Write: Developmentally Appropriate Practices for Young Children," Washington, D.C.: National Association for the Education of Young Children.

A Position Statement of the National Association for the Education of Young Children. "Developmentally Appropriate Practice in Early Childhood Programs Serving Children from Birth Through Age 8," NAEYC, Adopted 2009, accessed September 8, 2013, http://www.naeyc.org/positionstatements/dap.

Bardige, Betty S. and Marilyn M. Segal. 2005. *Building Literacy with Love: A Guide for Teachers and Caregivers of Children from Birth Through Age 5.* Washington, D.C.: Zero to Three.

Can You Read It Yes We Can, Inc. Accessed September 8, 2013. http://www.canyoureadityeswecan.com.

National Governors Association Center for Best Practices, Council of Chief State School Officers. 2010. *Common Core State Standards ELA.* Washington, D.C.: National Governors Association Center for Best Practices, Council of Chief State School Officers.

Neuman, S.B., C. Copple, and S. Bredekamp. 2000. "Learning to Read and Write: Developmentally Appropriate Practices for Young Children." Washington, D.C.: National Association for the Education of Young Children.

Owocki, Gretchen and Yetta Goodman. 2002. *Kid Watching: Documenting Children's Literacy Development.* Portsmouth, NH: Heinemann.

Snow, K. "Variation in Children's Experience of Kindergarten and the Common Core," Common Core Issue Brief NAEYC, November 2012, accessed September 8, 2013, http://www.naeyc.org/topics/common-core/issue-briefs.

Venn, E.C. and M.D. Jahn. 2003. T*eaching and Learning in Preschool: Using Individually Appropriate Practices in Early Childhood Literacy Instruction.* Newark, DE: International Reading Association.

Vygotsky, L.S. 1978. *Mind in Society: The Development of Higher Psychological Processes.* Cambridge, MA: Harvard University Press.

Yopp, R.H. and H.K. Yopp. 2000. "Sharing Informational Text with Young Children." *The Reading Teacher:* 53(5), 410–423.

Appendix

Kindergarten Information Sheet

Gaining an understanding of each student's life outside of school is very important to me. You are your child's first and most important teacher. Information that you can share with me will actually create a gateway to helping your child become the best learner possible. Therefore, I am asking you to forge a partnership of communication with me. Please provide as much information as you can about your child's interests, talents, and home life in answering the questions below. Be sure to circle the best way for me to reach you so that we can keep the lines of communication open. Feel free to contact me at _____ anytime with questions or concerns. It is a pleasure to be your partner in educating your child and I look forward to a great year!

Child's name _____ Prefers to be called _____

Language(s) Spoken at Home: Primary _____ Secondary _____

_____

Name of Parent/Guardian 1_____ Relationship to child _____

Home phone _____ Cell Phone _____

Work Phone _____ E-mail Address _____

*Please circle the best way to communicate with you from the list above.

_____

Name of Parent/Guardian 2_____ Relationship to child _____

Home phone _____ Cell Phone _____

Work Phone _____ E-mail Address _____

*Please circle the best way to communicate with you from the list above.

_____

Child lives with: (please check all that apply)

☐ Mother   ☐ Father   ☐ Stepmother   ☐ Stepfather   ☐ Brother(s)   ☐ Sister(s)

☐ Grandmother   ☐ Grandfather   ☐ Other(s)

_____

Child's siblings:

Name of brother or sister	Age/Grade	School
1 _____	_____	_____
2 _____	_____	_____
3 _____	_____	_____
4 _____	_____	_____

(Over) Canyoureadityeswecan.com

Tell Me More About Your Child

Important Medical Information/Allergies _____

_____

Does your child wear glasses? If so, for reading or distance and how often? _____

My child's interests include _____

_____

My child is very successful at _____

_____

My child struggles with _____

_____

My child's special qualities include _____

_____

My child usually approaches learning new things with: (Please check any of the following that apply)

☐ excitement   ☐ curiousity   ☐ confidence   ☐ anxiety   ☐ reluctance   ☐ other _____

Important information about our home life/culture I'd like to share_____

_____

Other information I'd like to share _____

_____

Goals I have for my child to achieve during kindergarten _____

_____

Thanks in advance for completing this form. I truly value any information you can provide as it will give me a "jump start" in getting to know your child and meeting his or her educational needs.

Parent Signature _____   Date _____

Please return by _____

Kindergarten
English Language Arts Standards

	Reading Standards: Literature
RL.K.1	I can ask and answer questions about text.
RL.K.2	I can retell stories with details.
RL.K.3	I can identify characters, setting, and major events in a story.
RL.K.4	I can ask and answer questions about words I do not know.
RL.K.5	I can recognize common types of text.
RL.K.6	I can identify the author and illustrator and describe what they do.
RL.K.7	I can match the illustration with its written part in the story.
RL.K.8	(does not apply)
RL.K.9	I can compare story characters and events.
RL.K.10	I can participate in group reading activities.
	Reading Standards: Informational Text
RI.K.1	I can ask and answer questions about informational text.
RI.K.2	I can identify the main idea and give details of the text.
RI.K.3	I can describe connections between individuals, events, and information in a text.
RI.K.4	I can ask and answer questions about words I do not know in text.
RI.K.5	I can identify the front cover, back cover, and title page of a book.
RI.K.6	I can identify the author and illustrator and describe what they do.
RI.K.7	I can match the illustration with its written part in the story.
RI.K.8	I can find evidence in a text to support the author's main idea.
RI.K.9	I can identify similarities and differences in texts.
RI.K.10	I can participate in group reading activities.
	Reading Standards: Foundational Skills
RF.K.1	I can show you how books work.
RF.K.1a	I can follow words from left to right, top to bottom, and page by page.
RF.K.1b	I know that words are written by using specific letters.
RF.K.1c	I know that words are separated by spaces in print.
RF.K.1d	I can name and recognize all capital and lowercase letters of the alphabet.
RF.K.2	I can play with words, syllables, and sounds.
RF.K.2a	I can tell you if two words rhyme, and I can make a rhyming word.
RF.K.2b	I can count, pronounce, blend, and segment syllables in words.
RF.K.2c	I can break apart and blend words using onsets and rimes.
RF.K.2d	I can isolate and pronounce the beginning, middle, and ending sounds in a word.
RF.K.2e	I can change beginning, middle, or ending sounds to make new words.
RF.K.3	I can decode words.
RF.K.3a	I can say the consonant letter sounds.
RF.K.3b	I can say the two sounds a vowel makes.
RF.K.3c	I can read sight words.
RF.K.3d	I can identify the letter sound that is different in words with similar spellings.
RF.K.4	I can read and make meaning.

Writing Standards	
W.K.1	I can write about my opinion about a book or topic.
W.K.2	I can write to give information about a topic.
W.K.3	I can write about an event or a series of events.
	(There is no W.K.4 standard as it starts in Grade 3)
W.K.5	I can edit my writing to make it better.
W.K.6	I can use digital tools to write.
W.K.7	I can participate in shared research and writing about a topic.
W.K.8	I can answer questions through remembering experiences and information.
Speaking and Listening Standards	
SL.K.1	I know how to be a superstar listener and speaker.
SL.K.1a	I can show that I am a superstar listener and speaker.
SL.K.1b	I take turns listening and speaking.
SL.K.2	I can ask and answer questions to help me understand information presented in ways other than by a speaker.
SL.K.3	I can ask and answer questions to help me understand information presented by a speaker.
SL.K.4	I can describe people, places, things, and events and give details.
SL.K.5	I can add drawings and pictures to make my presentations more understandable.
SL.K.6	I can be a superstar speaker.
Language Standards	
L.K.1	I am a superstar speaker and a superstar writer.
L.K.1a	I can write my capital and lowercase letters.
L.K.1b	I can speak and write using correct nouns and verbs.
L.K.1c	I can speak and write using correct plurals.
L.K.1d	I can speak and write using correct question words.
L.K.1e	I can speak and write using prepositions.
L.K.1f	I can share ideas in complete sentences.
L.K.2a-d	I can write sentences using capital letters, punctuation, and kindergarten spelling.
L.K.3	(Begins in grade 2)
L.K.4	I can learn the meaning of new words.
L.K.4a	I know that some words can have more than one meaning.
L.K.4b	I can be a detective to look for parts in words to help me understand their meaning.
L.K.5	I know to look for clues when I don't know the meaning of a new word.
L.K.5a	I can sort objects into categories.
L.K.5b	I can identify the opposite of a word.
L.K.5c	I can make connections between words I hear and read to my world.
L.K.5d	I can act out verbs that have similar meanings.
L.K.6	I can learn new words first and then use them in my speaking and writing.
	Notes:

Canyoureadityeswecan.com

ELA Assessment Checklist
Reading Standards: Literature

Student Name	RL.K.1 I can ask and answer questions about text.	RL.K.2 I can retell stories with details.	RL.K.3 I can identify characters, setting, and major events in a story.	RL.K.4 I can ask and answer questions about words I do not know.	RL.K.5 I can recognize common types of text.	RL.K.6 I can identify the author and illustrator and describe what they do.	RL.K.7 I can match the illustration with its written part in the story.	RL.K.9 I can compare story characters and events.	RL.K.10 I can participate in group reading activities.

Canyoureadityeswecan.com

ELA Assessment Checklist
Reading Standards: Informational Text

Student Name	RI.K.1 I can ask and answer questions about informational text.	RI.K.2 I can identify the main idea and give details of the text.	RI.K.3 I can describe connections between individuals, events, and information in a text.	RI.K.4 I can ask and answer questions about words I do not know in text.	RI.K.5 I can identify the front cover, back cover, and title page of a book.	RI.K.6 I can identify the author and illustrator and describe what they do.	RI.K.7 I can match the illustration with its written part in the story.	RI.K.8 I can find evidence in a text to support the author's main idea.	RI.K.9 I can identify similarities and differences in texts.	RI.K.10 I can participate in group reading activities.

Canyoureadityeswecan.com

ELA Assessment Checklist
Reading Standards: Foundational Skills (Page 1)

Student Name	RF.K.1 — I can show you how books work.	RF.K.1a — I can follow words from left to right, top to bottom, and page by page.	RF.K.1b — I know that words are written by using specific letters.	RF.K.1c — I know that words are separated by spaces in print.	RF.K.1d — I can name and recognize all capital and lowercase letters of the alphabet.	RF.K.2 — I can play with words, syllables, and sounds.	RF.K.2a — I can tell you if two words rhyme, and I can make a rhyming word.	RF.K.2b — I can count, pronounce, blend, and segment syllables in a word.	RF.K.2c — I can break apart and blend words using onsets and rimes.

Canyoureadityeswecan.com

ELA Assessment Checklist
Reading Standards: Foundational Skills (Page 2)

Student Name	RF.K.2d I can isolate and pronounce the beginning, middle, and ending sounds in words.	RF.K.2e I can change beginning, middle, or ending sounds to make new words.	RF.K.3 I can decode words.	RF.K.3a I can say the consonant letter sounds.	RF.K.3b I can say the two sounds a vowel makes.	RF.K.3c I can read sight words.	RF.K.3d I can identify the letter sound that is different in words with similar spellings.	RF.K.4 I can read and make meaning.

Canyoureadityeswecan.com

ELA Assessment Checklist
Writing Standards

Student Name	W.K.1 I can write about my opinion about a book or topic.	W.K.2 I can write to give information about a topic.	W.K.3 I can write about an event or a series of events.	W.K.5 I can edit my writing to make it better.	W.K.6 I can use digital tools to write.	W.K.7 I can participate in shared research and writing about a topic.	W.K.8 I can answer questions through remembering experiences and information.

Canyoureadityeswecan.com

ELA Assessment Checklist
Language Standards (Page 1)

Student Name	L.K.1 — I am a superstar speaker and a superstar writer.	L.K.1a — I can write my capital and lowercase letters.	L.K.1b — I can speak and write using correct nouns and verbs.	L.K.1c — I can speak and write using correct plurals.	L.K.1d — I can speak and write using correct question words.	L.K.1e — I can speak and write using prepositions.	L.K.1f — I can share ideas in complete sentences.	L.K.2a-d — I can write sentences using capital letters, punctuation, and kindergarten spelling.

Canyoureadityeswecan.com

ELA Assessment Checklist
Language Standards (Page 2)

Student Name	L.K.4 I can learn the meaning of new words.	L.K.4a I know that some words can have more than one meaning.	L.K.4b I can be a detective to look for parts in words to help me understand their meaning.	L.K.5 I know to look for clues when I don't know the meaning of a new word.	L.K.5a I can sort objects into categories.	L.K.5b I can identify the opposite of a word.	L.K.5c I can make connections between words I hear and read to my world.	L.K.5d I can act out verbs that have similar meanings.	L.K.6 I can learn new words first and then use them in my speaking and writing.

Canyoureadityeswecan.com

ELA Assessment Checklist
Speaking and Listening Standards

Student Name	SL.K.1 — I know how to be a superstar listener and speaker.	SL.K.1a — I can show that I am a superstar listener and speaker.	SL.K.1b — I take turns listening and speaking.	SL.K.2 — I can ask and answer questions to help me understand information presented in ways other than by a speaker.	SL.K.3 — I can ask and answer questions to help me understand information presented by a speaker.	SL.K.4 — I can describe people, places, things, and events and give details.	SL.K.5 — I can add drawings and pictures to make my presentations more understandable.	SL.K.6 — I can be a superstar speaker.

Canyoureadityeswecan.com

Question Response Sheet ☺

_____

Book Title: _____

I can write and/or draw about questions I have before, during, and after reading.

I can ask and answer questions about text.

Reading Literature RL.K. 1

Before ?

1

During ?

2

After ?

3

Canyoureadityeswecan.com

I can ask and answer questions about text.

Reading Literature RL.K. 1

Kindergarten Parents,

Learning to read is complex and takes much practice. Kindergartners need practice decoding words but they also need repeated opportunities to make meaning from text. They need to practice asking questions about books and making deeper connections. Young readers do not just naturally know how to comprehend text. They must be taught specific strategies that they can then practice with any book. This is one of the reasons why the partnership between parents and teachers is so important. We are introducing and practicing the following strategies in class and encourage you to try them at home too! You can use these ideas with any books you read to your children and with books they are beginning to read to you!

Questioning: Good readers constantly ask and answer questions as they read. To foster this behavior in young readers, parents should ask guiding questions <u>before, during, and after reading</u>. Before reading, ask children to make predictions or tell you what they already know about the topic. While the child is reading, adults should ask questions to check comprehension. After reading, ask questions to check for comprehension and to clear up misunderstandings. Children should also be encouraged to generate and answer their own questions about texts to eventually develop independent questioning skills. Be sure to ask the who, what, where, when and why questions. Don't forget to have your child tell you how they came to that answer. Where is the evidence from the text? How do you know?

Monitoring: Good readers constantly monitor their comprehension. They check to make sure that they understand what they are reading and if they do not, they adjust their approach to the text to ensure comprehension. Young readers often do not realize that they need to regularly "check in" with themselves while they are reading. Therefore, adults must help them develop self-monitoring skills. Prior to reading, parents should help children activate prior knowledge about the story's content. While the child is reading, help encourage reading comprehension by checking for understanding through questioning and connecting. Over time children will internalize these strategies and will be able to practice them independently.

Summarizing: When we read, we rarely sit down and formally create a summary of what we've read. Still, our minds store a picture of the key ideas in a text. Young readers need to be taught how to summarize what they have read. When readers are able to restate what they have read in their own words, they have truly understood it. Parents can foster this practice by asking children to summarize during and after reading. What was the author trying to teach us or tell us? How do you know?

Thanks so much for the at home help! The kindergartners will benefit from all of the support! Please let me know if you have questions.

_____

Kindergarten Teacher

Canyoureadityeswecan.com
Comprehension Bundle

I can draw and write about
the **plot** in a story!

Title of Book: _____

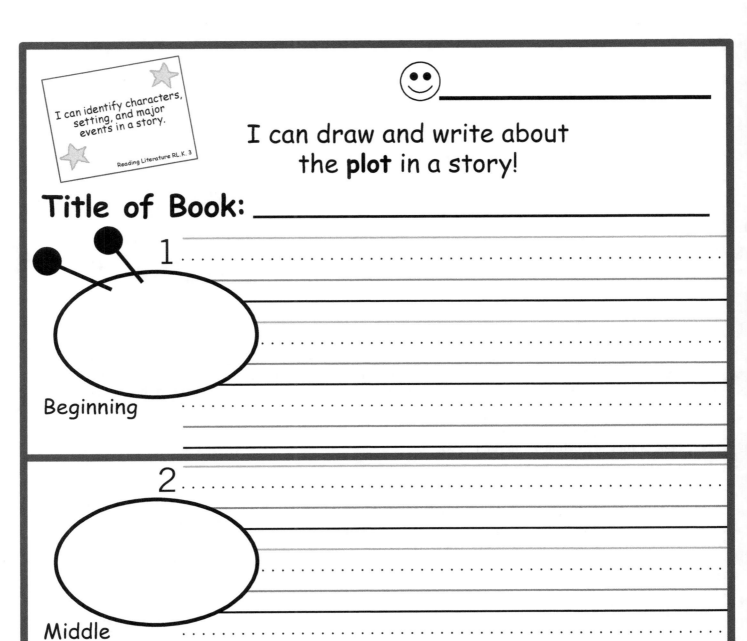

1

Beginning

2

Middle

3

End

I can identify characters, setting, and major events in a story.

Reading Literature RL.K. 3

Kindergarten Parents,

It is important that your child learns to identify the parts of a story to help him or her comprehend it. Specifically, young children need to be able to discuss **characters, setting,** and **plot.** You can help by reviewing these concepts at home before reading. Use the song posters below to encourage your child to sing about each skill. Each song is sung to the tune of "Mary Had a Little Lamb." Then after reading, ask your child to identify the characters, setting, and plot of the story. You can use this routine with any books you read to your child and with books he or she reads to you!

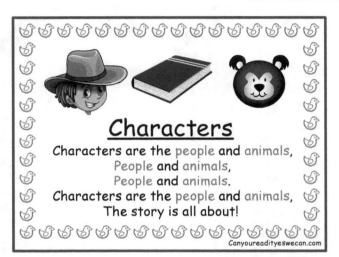

Characters

Characters are the people and animals,
People and animals,
People and animals.
Characters are the people and animals,
The story is all about!

Canyoureadityeswecan.com

Setting

Setting is the time and place,
Time and place,
Time and place.
Setting is the time and place,
The story is all about!

Canyoureadityeswecan.com

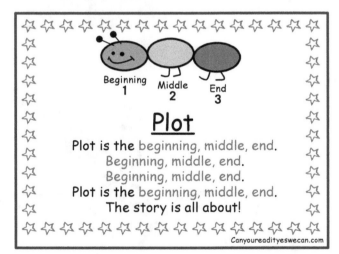

Plot

Plot is the beginning, middle, end.
Beginning, middle, end.
Beginning, middle, end.
Plot is the beginning, middle, end.
The story is all about!

Canyoureadityeswecan.com

Thanks so much for the at home help! The kindergartners will benefit from all of the support! Please let me know if you have questions!

_____

Kindergarten Teacher

Canyoureadityeswecan.com

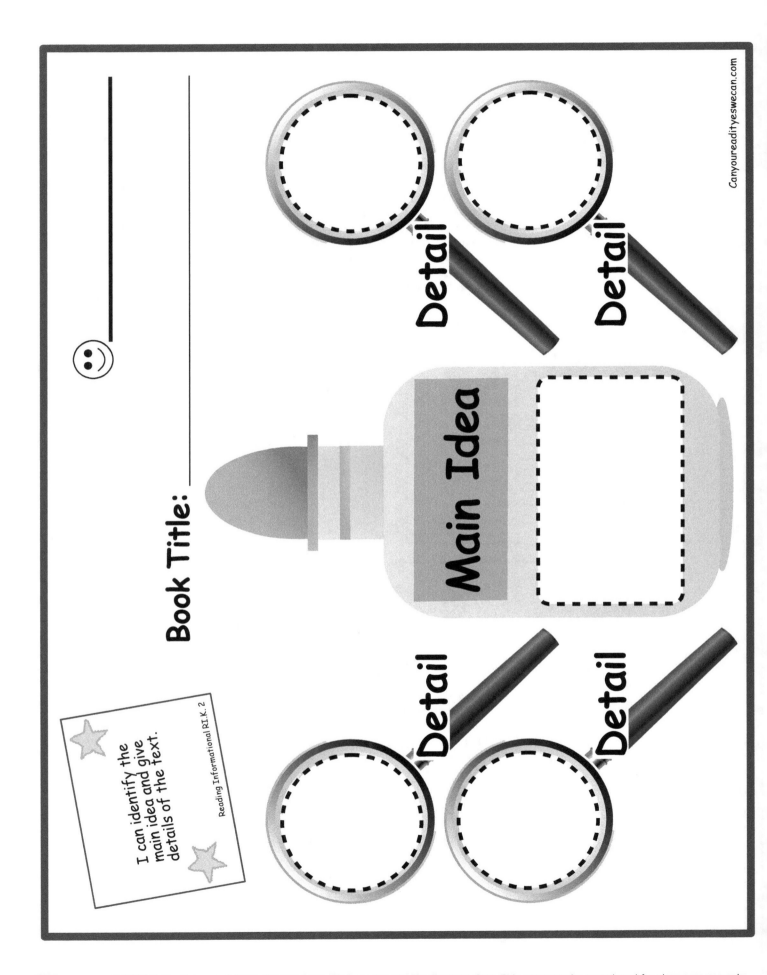

Book Title: _____

:)

Detail

Detail

Main Idea

Detail

Detail

I can identify the main idea and give details of the text.

Reading Informational RI.K. 2

I can identify the main idea and give details of the text.

Reading Informational RI.K. 2

Kindergarten Parents,

It is important that you read and discuss informational text with your child at home. Learning new facts helps children build vocabulary and make sense of the world around them. You can help broaden your child's background knowledge by exploring nonfiction books at home. Be sure to pick topics that are interesting. Also, it is very important to stop frequently when reading and discuss what can be learned on each page. Can your child find evidence in the text and illustrations to prove new learning? We have been practicing identifying the **main idea** and **details** in informational texts. The kindergartners know that the main idea is the "glue" that holds the book together and that the details support the main idea. We have learned the song below sung to the tune of "BINGO" to help us remember these important skills.

Before you read, ask your child to "switch on his or her searchlight" and become a detective for new facts. You will love the enthusiasm nonfiction reading will bring at home!

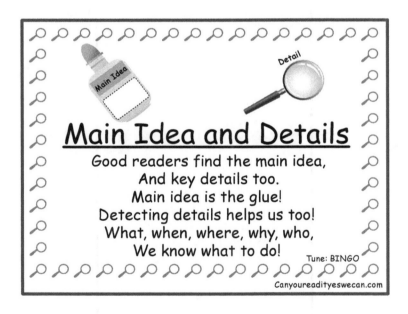

Main Idea and Details

Good readers find the main idea,
And key details too.
Main idea is the glue!
Detecting details helps us too!
What, when, where, why, who,
We know what to do!

Tune: BINGO

Canyoureadityeswecan.com

Thanks so much for the at home help! The kindergartners will benefit from all of the support! Please let me know if you have questions! Happy Reading!

_____

Kindergarten Teacher

Canyoureadityeswecan.com

Topic: _____

K⭐ What I know...	W? What I want to know...	L What I learned...

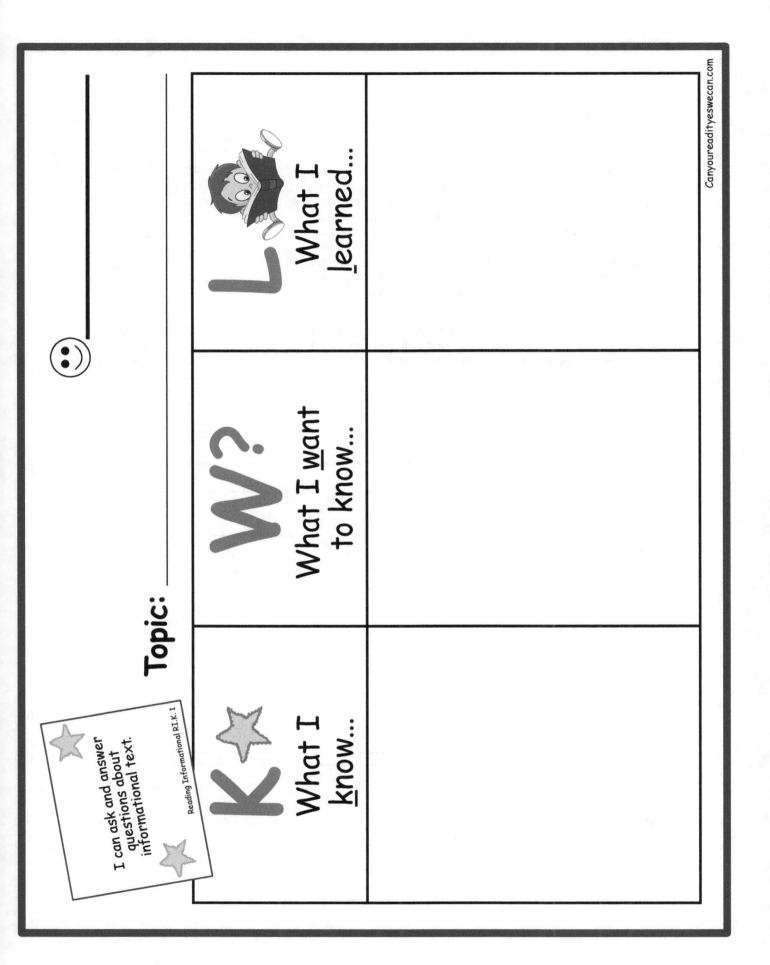

Topic: _____

K ⭐ What I <u>k</u>now...

W? What I <u>w</u>ant to know...

L What I <u>l</u>earned...

I can ask and answer questions about informational text.

Reading Informational RI.K.1

Canyoureadityeswecan.com

Kindergarten Parents,

It is important that you read and discuss informational text with your child at home. Learning new facts helps children build vocabulary and make sense of the world around them. You can help broaden your child's background knowledge by exploring nonfiction books at home. Kindergartners learn best when they can connect new knowledge to old experiences. They don't naturally know how to organize new learning in their brains so connecting gives them a "hook" to hang their new facts. In the classroom, we are using the KWL questioning strategy to help students organize their new learning. Below are some ways that you can practice asking and answering questions about informational text.

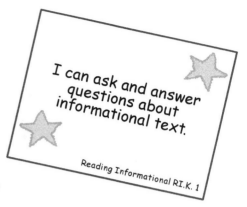

Before reading a new nonfiction book with your child, ask what he or she **already knows** about the topic and record responses in the **K column** of the KWL recording sheet. Then, ask about what he or she **wants to know** about the topic and record it in the **W column**. You can also add to any of the columns as you read. After reading the book, be sure to record what your child **learned** in the **L column**. This activity will encourage your child to be more interactive with the text and help him or her to comprehend the material on a deeper level.

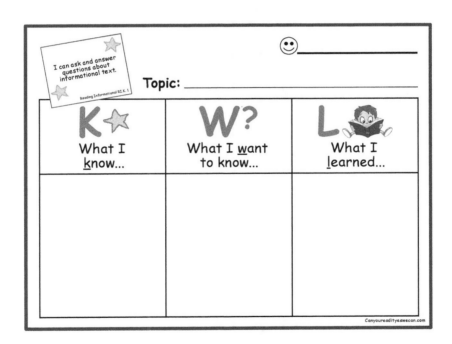

Thanks so much for the at home help! The kindergartners will benefit from all of the support!
Please let me know if you have questions! Happy Reading!

_____

Kindergarten Teacher

Canyoureadityeswecan.com

Kindergarten Parents,

In kindergarten, your child will be immersed in phonological/ phonemic awareness instruction. We teach the children to notice, think about, and work with (manipulate) sounds in spoken language. Research shows that phonemic awareness instruction helps children to read and write more fluently. When children read and write words more accurately and rapidly, it enables them to focus their attention on the meaning of words, which increases their comprehension. Therefore, it is important to expose children to phonemic awareness activities on a consistent basis. We will let you know what skills we are focusing on in class so that you can continue to practice them at home. It would be ideal if you would practice each skill (with 5 examples) at least 3–4 days per week. This should take about 10-15 minutes total each day. Since most of this is done verbally, you can enjoy practicing on long car rides or even while waiting in lines. Incorporating daily phonemic awareness practice into your family routines can be fun as well as beneficial! Thanks so much for the at home support!

I can play with words, syllables, and sounds.

Reading: Foundational Skills RF.K. 2

Counting Words in a Sentence

1. Give your child eight counters in a cup. You may use anything small and round for a counter like buttons, cheerios or goldfish.

2. Tell your child that you are going to play a counting game. **We're going to play a counting game. Let's practice counting using your special counters.** Have your child take one counter out of the cup at a time and place them in a line going straight across the table. **Look we have 8 counters.**

3. **Now we are going to practice counting objects. Each time we count something, we will push one of your counters in front of you forward like this.** Demonstrate pushing a counter forward. Always start with the counter on the left.

4. **So let's first practice counting windows. Each time I point at a window, push a counter forward in front of you.** Point at windows one by one and help students push counters into a row in front of them. (For the second or third time you play this game, try other objects in the room.)

5. **Did you know you can also count the words you hear in a sentence? Put your counters back in a straight line and I'll show you how. I'm going to say a sentence normally and then slowly. Here's the sentence: I see my mom.** Then slowly... **I   see   my   mom.** Model moving a counter forward slowly as you say each word. **Now you try.** Reset counters back in a straight line and repeat the sentence. **Push forward a counter each time I say a word.   I   see   my   mom.** Your child should have pushed 4 counters forward.

6. **Good! Now put your counters back and let's try another sentence.** Use sentences from the attached list.

7. You can also try movements instead of counters. Try clapping or jumping each time you hear a word instead of moving a counter. Just make sure to do only one motion per word.

8. **Happy Word Counting!**

Canyoureadityeswecan.com

Sentences that can be used for Word Counting:

1 word	2 words	3 words	4 words
Hi!	He fell.	You are nice.	The dog is brown.
Look	She sat.	The cat ran.	I can see it.
Wow	I cried.	He can play.	I like to sing.
Yes	Look here!	I can jump.	She is my friend.
No	Watch out!	I see you.	Can I go with?
Great	See me?	That is mine.	The snake is green.

5 words	6 words	7 words	8 words
The boy can jump high.	I like to see the pig.	It is fun to ride my bike.	He can go to the park with dad.
I see the blue bike.	The star is blue and red.	He can buy a new blue toy.	She can see the black dog by me.
Do you like the kite?	The girl can go to school.	The red kite can fly so high.	The pig will not get in the pen.
It is a red hen.	We will do our best work.	I can see the black cat run.	We can see the cold snow fall down.
Jim will eat the pie.	The fish can swim so fast.	The blue car can go so fast.	My dog will run to get the bone.
This was a fun day.	Do you see the big dog?	My dad can see the red cat.	My mom has a red and blue hat.

Canyoureadityeswecan.com

Kindergarten Parents,

We are practicing counting, segmenting, and blending syllables.
Kindergartners need to know how to count syllables orally.
A syllable is part of a word that contains one vowel sound.
For example, let's count the syllables in **September. Sep-** is
the first syllable, **-tem** is the second syllable, **-ber** is the third
syllable. Associating syllables with a beat can help students to
better learn the concept of syllables within words. Have your child
clap the three syllables in the word September. **Sep** (clap) **tem** (clap) **ber** (clap).
Try some of the activities listed below. There is a word list attached for you to use
as a resource for practicing syllables. Have fun!

Counting Syllables

1. **Can your child clap and count how many syllables are in a word?**
   For example: Say... butterfly. Your child should clap it back in syllables...
   but (clap) **ter** (clap) **fly** (clap). Butterfly has 3 syllables!

2. **Can your child identify the first and last syllable?**
   For example: Say... doghouse. Ask... First syllable? (dog) Last syllable? (house)
   Use 2 syllable words for practice.

3. **Can your child add syllables to the end or beginning of a word?**
   For example.. Say... sand, add box to the end. What is the new word? (sandbox) Say...
   house, add dog to the beginning. What is the new word? (doghouse)

4. **Can your child take away syllables to make new words?**
   For example: Say... rainbow, take away bow. What is the new word? (rain) Say...
   sunrise, take away sun. What is the new word? (rise)

5. **Can your child change syllables to make new words?**
   Say... rainbow, change bow to coat. What is the new word? (raincoat) Say...
   football, change foot to base. What is the new word? (baseball)

Remember this is all done verbally. There should be no print in front of your child.
It is a fun way to pass time while driving in the car or even waiting in line. Try a
combination of the above activities for about 10-15 minutes per day. Use the attached
list for ideas of words to use.

Canyoureadityeswecan.com

Word	Number of Syllables
boy	1
cat	1
me	1
sun	1
basket	2
airplane	2
table	2
bubble	2
wiggle	2
mailman	2
sunrise	2
sunset	2
nighttime	2
bedtime	2
lighthouse	2
nightlight	2
daytime	2
computer	3
butterfly	3
fantastic	3
hamburger	3
tomato	3
banana	3
dinosaur	3
information	4
pepperoni	4
motorcycle	4
macaroni	4
watermelon	4
caterpillar	4

Canyoureadityeswecan.com

Student:_____ Date:_____

Authentic Reading Assessment

Using any simple reader, mark the following criteria:

Skill	Satisfactory	Developing
Can the student identify the front cover of the book? Say, **Show me the front cover of the book.** (RI.K.5)	+	✓
Can the student identify the back cover of the book? Say, **Show me the back cover of the book.** (RI.K.5)	+	✓
Can the student identify the title of the book? Say, **Show me the title of the book.** (RI.K.5)	+	✓
Does the student know that print is read from left to right? Say, **Which way do I go? Where do I read next?** (RF.K.1a)	+	✓
Can the student identify a targeted letter in the book? Say, **Show me a letter____. Or What is this letter?** (RF.K.1d)	+	✓
Can the student identify a word in the book? Say, **Show me a word that you know and tell me what it is.** (RF.K.1c)	+	✓
Can the student identify an illustration in the book? Say, **Show me an illustration.** (RI.K.7)	+	✓
Does the student know the meaning of a period? Point to a period in the text. Say, **What is this and what do I use it for?** (L.K.2b)	+	✓
Does the student have one-to-one match with voice to print? Say, **Watch as I point and read the words.** Model pointing and reading the words for pages 2 and 3. Say, **Now it is your turn.** Point and read the rest of the book. (RI.K.10)	+	✓
Can the student make meaning of the text? Say, **Tell me, what was this book all about?** You might have to prompt with **tell me more** or **what else did you learn?** (RF.K.4)	+	✓

Canyoureadityeswecan.com

Notes:

Student: _____ Date: _____

Authentic Reading Assessment: Sight Words

Using any of the books to mark the following criteria:

Skill	Satisfactory	Developing
Can the student identify the front cover of the book? Say, **Show me the front cover of the book.** (RI.K.5)	**+**	✓
Can the student identify the back cover of the book? Say, **Show me the back cover of the book.** (RI.K.5)	**+**	✓
Can the student identify the title of the book? Say, **Show me the title of the book.** (RI.K.5)	**+**	✓
Does the student know that print is read from left to right? Say, **Which way do I go? Where do I read next?** (RF.K.1a)	**+**	✓
Can the student identify a letter in the book? Say, **Show me a letter that you know and tell me what it is.** (RF.K.1d)	**+**	✓
Can the student identify a word in the book? Say, **Show me a word that you know and tell me what it is.** (RF.K.1c)	**+**	✓
Can the student tell what an illustration depicts? Say, **Describe what this illustration tells us about.** (RI.K.7)	**+**	✓
Does the student know the meaning of a period? Point to a period in the text. Say, **What is this called and what do I use it for?** (L.K.2b)	**+**	✓
Can the student identify the **targeted** sight word in the book? (Use a flash card or the book to point to the word and have student identify targeted sight word.) (RF.K.3c)	**+**	✓
Does the student have one-to-one match with voice to print? Say, **Watch as I point and read the words.** Model pointing and reading the words for pages 2 and 3. Say, **Now it is your turn. Point and read the rest of the book.** (RI.K.10)	**+**	✓
Can the student make meaning of the text? Say, **Tell me, what was this book all about?** You might have to prompt with **tell me more** or what else did you learn? (RF.K.4)	**+**	✓

Canyoureadityeswecan.com

Notes:

Student:_____ Date: _____

Authentic Writing Assessment

For use with any writing paper. Mark the following criteria:

Skill	Satisfactory	Developing
Did the student begin **writing** (an opinion or information) after the prompt or was extra support needed to generate ideas? (W.K.1-2)	+	✓
Did the student use a correct **pencil grip** and form letters correctly? (L.K.1a)	+	✓
Did the student use **directionality** when writing? (Start at the left and go to the right and start from the top to the bottom.)	+	✓
Did the student write **more** than one sentence about the topic?	+	✓
Did the student use a **capital letter** at the beginning of the sentences? (L.K.2a)	+	✓
Did the student use correct **spacing** within sentences?	+	✓
Did the student use appropriate **punctuation** at the end of sentences? (L.K.2b)	+	✓
Did the student use correct spelling when writing **high frequency words**?	+	✓
Did the student attempt to use **developmental spelling** on non-high frequency words? (L.K.2c-d)	+	✓
Did the student's **illustration** reflect the sentences written?	+	✓
Was the student able to **read** the sentences back and **construct meaning** from his or her work?	+	✓

Canyoureadityeswecan.com

Notes:

I am a superstar writer!

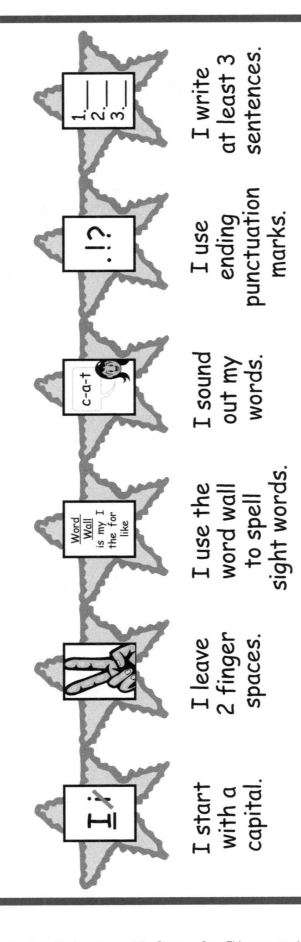

I start with a capital.

I leave 2 finger spaces.

I use the word wall to spell sight words.

I sound out my words.

I use ending punctuation marks.

I write at least 3 sentences.

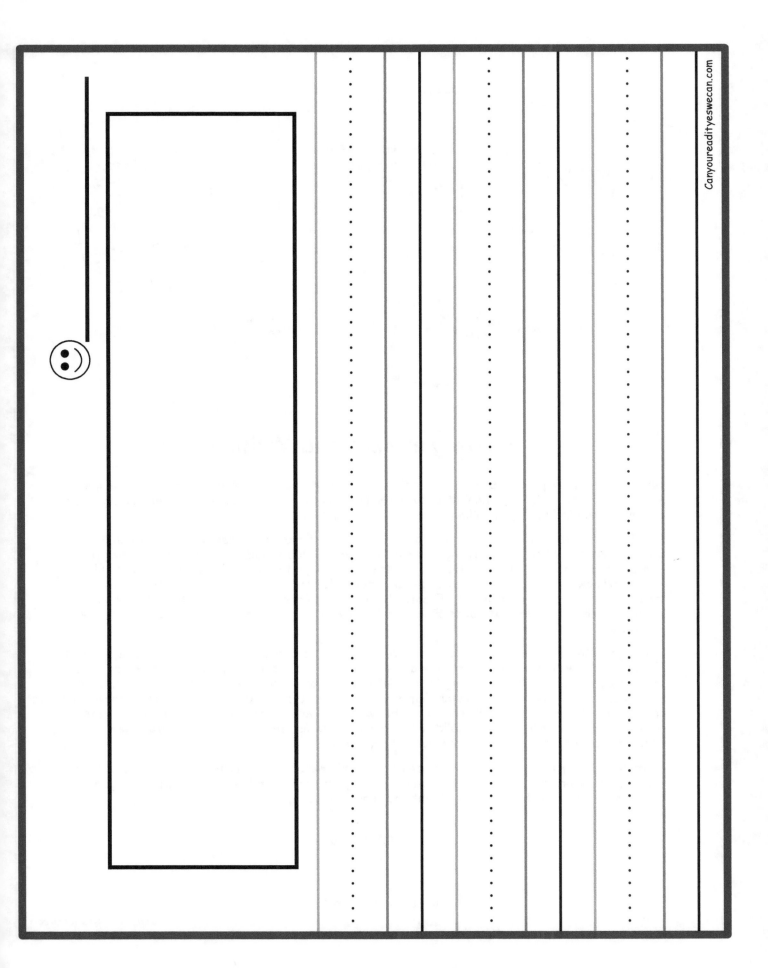

Canyoureadityeswecan.com

I can share my ideas in complete sentences.

Language L.K. 1f

I can write about my opinion about a book or topic.

Writing W.K. 1

I can write sentences using capital letters, punctuation, and kindergarten spelling.

Language L.K. 2a-d

I can write my capital and lowercase letters.

Language L.K. 1a

I can edit my writing to make it better.

Writing W.K. 5

Kindergartners and Writing

Writing is a very important part of your child's literacy development. In kindergarten, we began writing on the first day of school. We have been praising the students for all of their writing attempts and celebrating by calling them "superstar writers."

It is important to realize that learning to write is a developmental process that takes much practice. Each child explores writing on his or her own timetable. Most children begin writing by expressing themselves through illustrating. Next, they begin to add random scribbles that only they know how to "read." Then, they begin to copy words from signs, books, and so on as they identify words in their environment. Eventually, kindergartners start to use letters and sounds as they attempt to sound out words. Finally, they are able to compose full sentences that include spacing and punctuation.

This writing journey requires repeated practice, patience, encouragement, and acceptance. At first glance, your child's attempts at writing may be confusing. We encourage parents to step back and let your child read his or her writing to you. Taking a look at your kindergartner's writing through his or her lens will "unlock the mystery" of meaning. Don't worry about perfect spelling, handwriting or punctuation. Just let your child read his or her writing to you. Simply celebrate his or her efforts in expressing thoughts on paper. Build confidence and enthusiasm. Writing is powerful when children understand its ability to communicate meaning.

Writing with your kindergartner should be an enjoyable experience. Writing should not be seen as just homework or deskwork. Writing should become part of your child's daily "lifework." Together we can help your child become a confident and capable kindergarten writer.

Happy Writing!

_____

Kindergarten Teacher

Canyoureadityeswecan.com

Parents can help kindergartners grow as writers by giving them lots of opportunities to write and lots of positive feedback. Here are some ideas:

✎ Help your child understand that writing is simply expressing your thoughts on paper. Writing is talking with your pencil. Model saying a sentence out loud and then writing it on paper.

✎ Pick a writing topic that is important and interesting to your child. At first, he or she might write just a single word or sentence. Be all accepting and encouraging. Try making homemade journals from blank stapled sheets of paper. Your child will love writing about his or her daily adventures.

✎ Provide practice writing capital and lowercase letters to increase writing fluency. Students who can easily write their letters can focus on expressing their ideas without stressing about handwriting. Use fun materials, such as sidewalk chalk, finger paint, oil pastels, paint, and so on to strengthen fine motor skills.

✎ Encourage your child to take the risk to sound out words and sentences. Kindergartners are not expected to write like adults. They use their kindergarten spelling. Kindergarten spellers stretch out their words like bubble gum and listen for sounds. Then they write the letters for the sounds they heard. For example, a child might write p-l-a for play because these are the sounds that are heard. The more children read and write, the more words they will begin to spell the grown-up way. Writing is a great way to practice phonics skills.

✎ Keep a list of sight words near your child's writing area. Encourage him or her to refer to this list when spelling simple sight words. All other words should be sounded out.

✎ Kindergartners need to be shown how to put "two finger" spaces between words. Sound out a sentence with your child. Stop as needed and put your two fingers down to represent spacing between words. Explain that writing without spacing runs together and can't be understood.

✎ Help your child remember to end each sentence with a punctuation mark. We have talked about using a period for a telling sentence, a question mark when asking a question, and an exclamation mark when your sentence is exciting.

✎ Encourage students to write and illustrate with lots of detail. Good writers use colorful words and detailed descriptions when they write. Writing and illustrations should match.

✎ Your kindergartner needs LOTS and LOTS of opportunities to write. Provide many different reasons to write including grocery lists, letters, observations, weather reports, to-do lists, stories, wish lists, and so on. Also provide a variety of audiences. Your child will LOVE to share his or her writing with brothers, sisters, grandparents, teddy bears, and even the dog. The more kindergartners write the better writers they become.

_____

Look! I circled all of the stars I earned with my writing.

I am a superstar writer!

| I start with a capital. | I leave 2 finger spaces. | I use the word wall to spell sight words. | I sound out my words. | I use ending punctuation marks. | I write at least 3 sentences. |

I can circle the parts I **need to work on** in my writing.

I need to...

Canyoureadityeswecan.com

I am a Superstar Speaker

Look at audience

Use just the right volume and speed

Stand nicely

Stay on topic

I am a Superstar Listener

Eyes on the speaker

Ears listening quietly

Mouth closed

Hands and feet to yourself

Raise hand to ask questions

Kindergarten Parents,

Children need to successfully use speaking and listening to explore new ideas and connect them with old experiences. Kindergartners learn so much about themselves and others when they talk to one another. Your child is learning how to be a superstar listener and a superstar speaker in school. We have been using the poster pictured below in the classroom as a visual reminder of what to do when you are speaking and when you are listening. We have also been practicing taking turns when we talk. Talking friends decide who gets to be the speaker first and who gets to be the listener first. Then, they take turns.

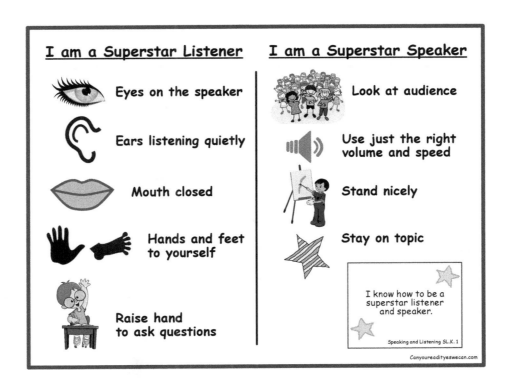

Please encourage superstar listening and speaking at home too! Thanks so much for all of the help. The kindergartners will benefit from your support! Please let me know if you have questions.

_____

Kindergarten Teacher

Canyoureadityeswecan.com

Maupin House *by*
capstone®
professional

At Maupin House by Capstone Professional, we continue to look for professional development resources that support grades K–8 classroom teachers in areas, such as these:

Literacy
Content-Area Literacy
Assessment
Technology
Standards-Based Instruction
Classroom Management

Language Arts
Research-Based Practices
Inquiry
Differentiation
School Safety
School Community

If you have an idea for a professional development resource, visit our Become an Author website at:

http://maupinhouse.com/index.php/become-an-author

There are two ways to submit questions and proposals.

1. You may send them electronically to:
http://maupinhouse.com/index.php/become-an-author

2. You may send them via postal mail. Please be sure to include a self-addressed stamped envelope for us to return materials.
Acquisitions Editor
Capstone Professional
1 N. LaSalle Street, Suite 1800
Chicago, IL 60602